Poison Ivy

This weed (above) causes an itchy rash if you touch it. Poison ivy grows as a vine or shrub. Try to remember what the leaves look like, and do not touch them or other parts of the plant. If you do touch poison ivy, washing your hands as soon as possible may reduce the itching. Your local drugstore will have various remedies that will help.

World Book's

SCIENCE & NATURE GUIDES

TREES

OF THE UNITED STATES AND CANADA

World Book, Inc.
a Scott Fetzer company
Chicago

Scientific names

In this book, after the common name of a tree is given, that tree's scientific name usually appears. Scientific names are put into a special type of lettering, called italic, *which looks like this.*

The first name in a scientific name is the genus. A genus consists of very similar groups, but the members of these different groups usually cannot reproduce with one another. The second name given is the species. Every known organism (life form) belongs to a particular species. Members of a species can reproduce with one another, and the young grow up to look very much like the parents.

A scientific name is the same worldwide. This helps scientists and students to know which organism is being discussed, since an organism may have many different common names.

Therefore, when you see a name like *Fraxinus americana*, you know that the genus is *Fraxinus* and the species is *americana* for the white ash (see page 25).

Respecting the Forest

1 **Never break branches off a living tree** or carve words or pictures in its bark.

2 **Don't climb trees;** you may damage them or hurt yourself.

3 **Ask your parents only to light fires in a designated picnic area** in a woods or forest, and to use the fireplaces provided.

4 **Ask permission** before exploring or crossing private property.

5 **Stay on the footpaths as much as possible** and don't trample the undergrowth.

6 **Leave fences and gates as you found them.**

7 **Wear long pants, a hat, and a long-sleeved shirt** in tick country.

This edition published in the United States of America by World Book, Inc., Chicago.

WORLD BOOK and the GLOBE DEVICE are registered trademarks or trademarks of World Book, Inc.

World Book, Inc.
233 North Michigan Avenue
Chicago, IL 60601 USA

For information about other World Book publications, visit our Web site **http://www.worldbook.com,** or call **1-800-WORLDBK (967-5325).** For information about sales to schools and libraries, call **1-800-975-3250 (United States); 1-800-837-5365 (Canada).**

Library of Congress Cataloging-in-Publication Data

Trees of the United States and Canada.
    p. cm. — (World Book's science & nature guides)
    Includes bibliographical references (p.).
    ISBN 0-7166-4219-0 — ISBN 0-7166-4208-5 (set)
    1. Trees—United States—Identification—Juvenile literature. 2. Trees—Canada—Identification—Juvenile literature. I. World Book, Inc. II. Series.

QK115 .T743 2005
582.16'097—dc22
                                                    2004041972

Edited text and captions based on *Trees of North America* by Alan Mitchell. Habitat paintings and headbands by Antonia Phillips; identification and activities illustrations by Richard Coombes.

For World Book:
General Managing Editor: Paul A. Kobasa
Editorial: Shawn Brennan, Maureen Liebenson, Christine Sullivan
Research: Madolynn Cronk, Lynn Durbin, Cheryl Graham, Karen McCormack, Loranne Shields, Hilary Zawidowski
Librarian: Jon Fjortoft
Permissions: Janet Peterson
Graphics and Design: Sandra Dyrlund, Anne Fritzinger
Indexing: Aamir Burki, David Pofelski
Pre-press and Manufacturing: Carma Fazio, Steve Hueppchen, Jared Svoboda, Madelyn Underwood
Text Processing: Curley Hunter, Gwendolyn Johnson
Proofreading: Anne Dillon

Printed in China
1 2 3 4 5 6 7 8 9 10 09 08 07 06 05 04

Contents

Entries *like this* indicate pages featuring projects you can do!

Introduction To Trees

There are trees everywhere, not just in woods and the countryside, but in urban parks, gardens, and yards as well. In the countryside you are most likely to see native trees. These trees grow naturally from their own seed and were not introduced into that area by humans.

You can see native trees in cities too, but these trees have usually been planted by people. Many non-native trees are planted as well. Most have been introduced (brought as seeds from other countries), and a few are crosses between different kinds of related trees.

The more you know about trees, the more interesting they are. This book will help you recognize more than their leaves. In winter you can look at their bark and buds. In spring you can watch certain types of trees flower. This flowering enables them to produce seeds and fruits in summer and fall. (Some trees, like conifers, produce seeds without flowering.)

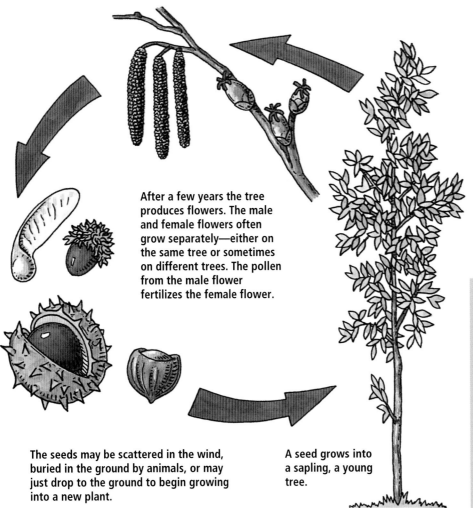

After a few years the tree produces flowers. The male and female flowers often grow separately—either on the same tree or sometimes on different trees. The pollen from the male flower fertilizes the female flower.

The seeds may be scattered in the wind, buried in the ground by animals, or may just drop to the ground to begin growing into a new plant.

A seed grows into a sapling, a young tree.

The life of a flowering tree

Some introduced trees become naturalized—that is, they grow naturally from seed like native trees. A few introduced trees have to be grafted on to the stem of a native tree, but most are raised from seeds or cuttings, like the natives.

This mark on the trunk shows where one tree has been grafted, or joined, on to the stem of another. Grafting is necessary when a tree, like a Japanese cherry, is incapable of producing a seed.

How to use this book

You can use this book to find out more about trees that you already recognize, or to identify a tree you do not know.

1 **Decide what kind of tree it is**—broadleaf, ornamental, evergreen, or coniferous. You will find descriptions of them at the start of each section. The tree on the left is coniferous, so turn to pages 48–77.

2 **Where is it growing?** If it is growing wild in the countryside, it is most likely to be found in the first section. If it has obviously been planted for decoration, start looking in the second section. Only broadleaf trees that keep their leaves all winter are shown in the evergreen section.

3 **Check what shape the leaves are.** The conifer has single needles, so look through those trees, checking the shape of the tree and the bark against those illustrated. You will find that the tree on the left is a Douglas-fir (see page 67).

4 **If you decide that the tree has been specially planted,** but you cannot find it in the second section, try the first section. Here the trees are arranged according to the shape of their leaves.

Top-of-page Picture Bands

Each group of trees has a different picture band at the top of the page—they are shown below.

Broadleaf Trees

Ornamental Trees

Evergreen Trees

Conifers

What To Look For

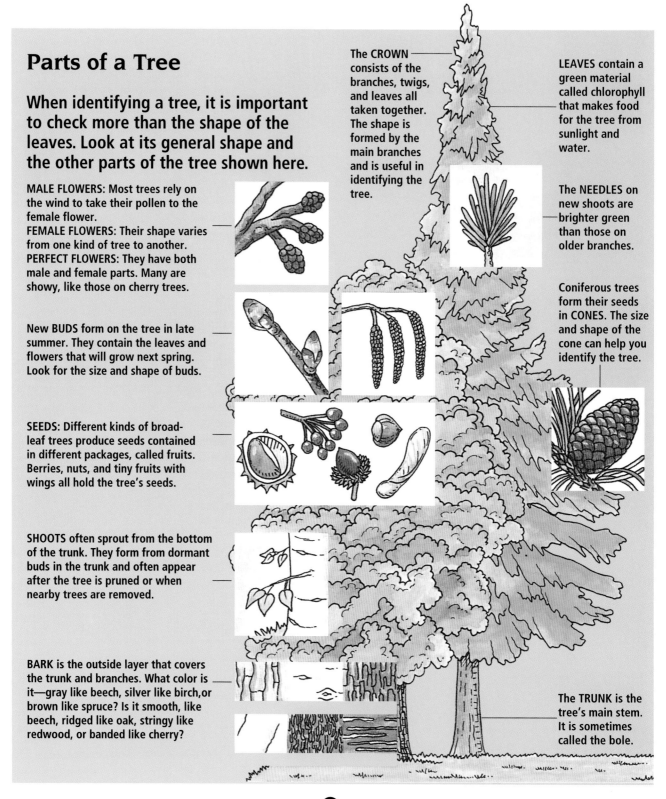

Parts of a Tree

When identifying a tree, it is important to check more than the shape of the leaves. Look at its general shape and the other parts of the tree shown here.

MALE FLOWERS: Most trees rely on the wind to take their pollen to the female flower.
FEMALE FLOWERS: Their shape varies from one kind of tree to another.
PERFECT FLOWERS: They have both male and female parts. Many are showy, like those on cherry trees.

New **BUDS** form on the tree in late summer. They contain the leaves and flowers that will grow next spring. Look for the size and shape of buds.

SEEDS: Different kinds of broad-leaf trees produce seeds contained in different packages, called fruits. Berries, nuts, and tiny fruits with wings all hold the tree's seeds.

SHOOTS often sprout from the bottom of the trunk. They form from dormant buds in the trunk and often appear after the tree is pruned or when nearby trees are removed.

BARK is the outside layer that covers the trunk and branches. What color is it—gray like beech, silver like birch, or brown like spruce? Is it smooth, like beech, ridged like oak, stringy like redwood, or banded like cherry?

The **CROWN** consists of the branches, twigs, and leaves all taken together. The shape is formed by the main branches and is useful in identifying the tree.

LEAVES contain a green material called chlorophyll that makes food for the tree from sunlight and water.

The **NEEDLES** on new shoots are brighter green than those on older branches.

Coniferous trees form their seeds in **CONES**. The size and shape of the cone can help you identify the tree.

The **TRUNK** is the tree's main stem. It is sometimes called the bole.

Shape of Trees

The overall shape of a tree is a useful clue to its identity. Here are some things to look for:

Many conifers are themselves cone-shaped, narrowing to a point at the top.

Some broad-leaf trees are also tall and narrow.

This tree has a spreading crown.

Do the branches arch downward like a basswood—or point upward like a maple?

Many trees have a weeping form.

Shape of Leaves

When trying to identify a tree, the first thing to look at is the shape of its leaves.

A pine has thin, sharp leaves, called needles.

A beech can have round leaves.

A cherry has toothed, oval leaves.

Some oaks have lobed leaves.

A sycamore has palmate leaves.

A mountain ash has compound leaves made up of several leaflets.

Arrangement of Needles

Look at the way the needles of a coniferous tree grow—they are an important clue to identifying it.

The leaves of a cypress enclose the branch like scales.

Spruce needles grow singly along the branch.

Scotch pine needles grow in pairs.

Larch needles form rosettes.

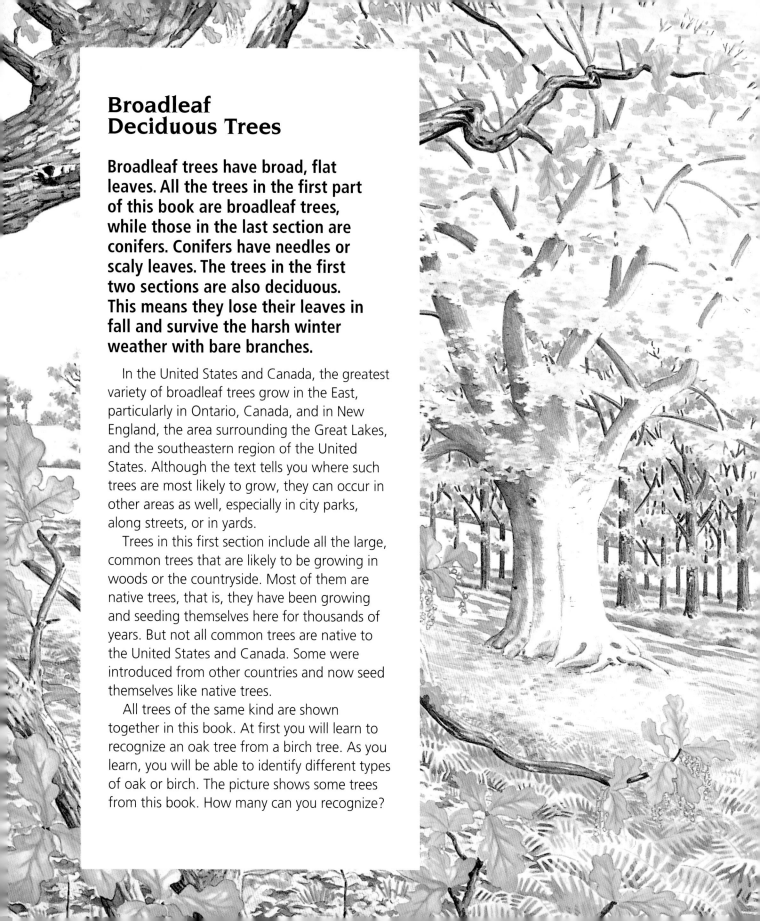

Broadleaf Deciduous Trees

Broadleaf trees have broad, flat leaves. All the trees in the first part of this book are broadleaf trees, while those in the last section are conifers. Conifers have needles or scaly leaves. The trees in the first two sections are also deciduous. This means they lose their leaves in fall and survive the harsh winter weather with bare branches.

In the United States and Canada, the greatest variety of broadleaf trees grow in the East, particularly in Ontario, Canada, and in New England, the area surrounding the Great Lakes, and the southeastern region of the United States. Although the text tells you where such trees are most likely to grow, they can occur in other areas as well, especially in city parks, along streets, or in yards.

Trees in this first section include all the large, common trees that are likely to be growing in woods or the countryside. Most of them are native trees, that is, they have been growing and seeding themselves here for thousands of years. But not all common trees are native to the United States and Canada. Some were introduced from other countries and now seed themselves like native trees.

All trees of the same kind are shown together in this book. At first you will learn to recognize an oak tree from a birch tree. As you learn, you will be able to identify different types of oak or birch. The picture shows some trees from this book. How many can you recognize?

Birch, Alder, & Beech

Alders and birches have simple, toothed leaves. Look at the bark to tell them apart.

Speckled Alder
(Alnus rugosa)

Alders like wet ground, so they are most likely to be growing along the edges of lakes and streams, or in swampy ground. The bark is gray and smooth. There are tiny flowers in early spring before the leaves come out. The drooping catkins (tassellike flower clusters) are male flowers. Female flowers are small cones, which become hard and black as they swell to about half an inch (13 millimeters) long during summer. Deer and moose may hide in thick clumps of alder. Birds also feed on the seeds.

Variation of European gray alder
Found across Canada and northeastern U.S.
Grows up to 20 ft (6 m) tall
Leaves 2–4 in (5–10 cm) long.

Paper Birch
(Betula papyrifera)

You can tell many birches at once from their silvery-white bark and elegant shape. The paper birch gets its name from the bark, which peels off in papery strips to show the orange layer beneath. Look for the flowers in early spring. The yellowy catkins are male. The short, green catkins which grow just behind them are female flowers. In fall, the tree has hanging cones of winged nutlets. The wood of the paper birch is made into ice cream sticks, broom handles, and toys. American Indians used it to make their canoes.

Native to Canada
and the northern U.S.
Grows up to 80 ft (24 m) tall
Leaves 2–4 in (5–10 cm) long

Gray Birch
(Betula populifolia)

Gray birches grow along roadsides in woodlands across eastern Canada and the northeastern United States. The tree has long-tipped triangular leaves, which are smaller than those of the paper birch. Look too for the dark, V-shaped patches on the white bark just below the drooping branches.

Nova Scotia and Quebec to northern Virginia
Grows up to 40 ft (12 m) tall
Leaves 2–3 in (5–7.5 cm) long

Beeches often have oval, toothed leaves. Lindens and basswoods have heart-shaped, toothed leaves.

Little-leaf Linden
(Tilia cordata)

Lindens and basswoods belong to the same family and so have similar leaves and fruits. The little-leaf linden can be recognized by its small leaves and its starry, yellow flowers, which grow in clusters.
Introduced from Europe Planted in many cities in southern Canada and the northern and eastern U.S.—Grows up to 60 ft (18 m) tall Leaves 1½–3 in (4–7.5 cm) long

European Beech
(Fagus sylvatica)

This beech is easy to recognize for its dark, purplish-black leaves. In summer it gives abundant shade; it produces beechnuts in fall like the American beech. It is sometimes called copper beech or purple beech.
Introduced from Europe Planted in the northeastern and Pacific U.S. Grows up to 70 ft (21 m) tall Leaves 2–4 in (5–10 cm) long

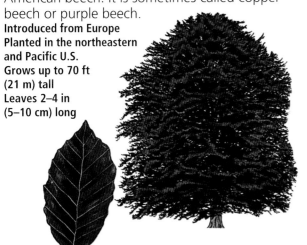

Basswood
(Tilia americana)

Basswood, or linden, is sometimes called the "beetree" because it attracts so many bees when it flowers in early summer. The small, yellow-white flowers hang in clusters and smell sweet. In autumn, they turn into clusters of small, hard fruit. As the tree gets older, the smooth, dark gray bark becomes ridged and scaly. The wood is soft and light.
Native to southern Canada and the eastern U.S.—Grows up to 100 ft (30 m) tall Leaves 3–6 in (7.5–15 cm) long

American Beech
(Fagus grandifolia)

Even old beeches have smooth, light gray bark. The flowers emerge just as the leaves are opening. The male flowers are round, yellowish balls that hang on slender stalks. The female flowers are very small and are harder to spot. In fall, the flowers develop into beechnuts, protected in a prickly case. Squirrels, raccoons, bears, and game birds eat the nuts, and so do humans.
Native to southeastern Canada and the eastern U.S. Grows up to 75 ft (23 m) tall Leaves 2¼–5 in (5.5–12.5 cm) long

Elms & Poplars

Elms have toothed, oval-shaped leaves. Three other trees from the elm family are shown on page 28.

Cedar Elm
(Ulmus crassifolia)

Cedar elms are common native elms in eastern Texas and the Southwest of the United States. They are often planted there to give shade. Their leaves are smaller than those of other native elms and are leathery and thick.

Native to extreme southwestern U.S.
Grows up to 80 ft (24 m) tall
Leaves 1–2 in (2.5–5 cm) long

Slippery Elm
(Ulmus rubra)

Slippery elm gets its name from its sticky, aromatic inner bark, which can be dried and made into cough medicine. This elm features very rough leaves and dark brown bark with deep furrows.

Native to southern Canada and the eastern U.S.
Grows up to 70 ft (21 m) tall
Leaves 4–7 in (10–18 cm) long

American Elm
(Ulmus americana)

An American elm is recognizable by the shape of its broad, rounded crown. It is flat on top with branches that droop at the ends. The trees' seeds form in spring. These seeds are flat and oval, and have a deep notch where the pointed wings meet. The wood is used for furniture and containers. American elms used to be very common on lawns and city streets, but Dutch elm disease, spread by bark beetles, has killed many of these trees.

Native to the central and eastern U.S. and Canada
Grows up to 100 ft (30 m) tall
Leaves 3–6 in (7.5–15 cm) long

These trees belong to the poplars, which are part of the willow family. They have triangular or rounded, toothed leaves.

Balsam Poplar
(Populus balsamifera)

The leaves of the balsam poplar are shiny green above and whitish below. Even before the leaves emerge, the tree can be recognized by the sweet smell of its sticky buds. The flowers are brownish catkins, which on female trees develop into cottony seeds.
Native across Canada and the northern U.S.
Grows up to 80 ft (24 m) tall
Leaves 3–5 in (7.5–12.5 cm) long

Quaking Aspen
(Populus tremuloides)

Quaking aspens get their name from the movement of their leaves. Even the smallest breeze makes them flutter. In fall the trees look quite spectacular as the leaves turn a brilliant golden-yellow. Beavers, rabbits, and other animals like to feed on the bark, leaves, and buds. The scratch marks of a bear might be seen on the trunk.
Native in all North America, from Labrador and Alaska, down the Rocky Mountains to Mexico
Grows up to 70 ft (21 m) tall
Leaves 1¼–3 in (3–7.5 cm) long

Eastern Cottonwood
(Populus deltoides)

Cottonwoods get their name from their cottony, white seeds. Before the leaves open, long, sticky buds and brown catkins emerge. Male and female flowers grow on separate trees. The seed capsules give the tree another of its names, necklace poplar, because they look like strings of beads. When the capsules open, the tree releases masses of "cotton," which blows everywhere.
Native throughout southern Canada, and the eastern and central U.S.
Grows up to 100 ft (30 m) tall
Leaves 3–7 in (7.5–18 cm) long

Lombardy Poplar
(Populus nigra var. italica)

The tall, thin shape of this tree makes it one of the easiest to recognize. The trees are often planted in a line to form a windbreak. Lombardy poplars are male trees. They have dark red catkins in early spring, but no seeds. New trees are produced by taking a cutting or root sprout from an existing tree.
Introduced from Europe
Planted throughout the U.S.
Grows up to 60 ft (18 m) tall
Leaves 1½–3 in (4–7.5 cm) long

Hornbeams & Willows

Hornbeams, or ironwoods, have toothed, simple leaves with deep veins. They are similar to birch and beech leaves, but are duller green.

European Hornbeam
(Carpinus betulus)

Although the American hornbeam looks more spectacular in fall, the European hornbeam is usually planted in parks and gardens in its stead. It can be trimmed into hedge form. Trees mature from a pyramidal to a rounded shape. Buds can be seen in winter, curving back around the stem.

Introduced from Europe
Planted for ornament, mainly in the east
Grows up to 80 ft (24 m) tall
Leaves 3–4¾ in (7.5–12 cm) long

Hop Hornbeam
(Ostrya virginiana)

This tree takes its name from the clusters of fruit, which look something like the hops with which beer is flavored. The clusters drop from the tree in winter and provide food for wildlife. These conelike clusters are a good way of identifying the tree. Each brown nutlet is held in a papery, light brown sack. The tree is sometimes called ironwood, after its tough, hard wood, which is used for tool handles and fence posts.

Native to southeastern Canada and the eastern U.S.
Grows up to 50 ft (15 m) tall
Leaves 2–5 in (5–12.5 cm) long

American Hornbeam
(Carpinus caroliniana)

The American hornbeam is sometimes called bluebeech or waterbeech, because the leaves and blue-gray bark look like those of beech. They are much smaller than beech trees, however, and often grow only as a shrub. In fall their leaves turn orange and red. Clusters of tiny, green nutlets held in three-pointed bracts (scalelike leaves) develop in late summer. The wood is very tough and hard and is used for tool handles.

Native to southeastern Canada and the eastern U.S.
Grows up to 30 ft (9 m) tall
Leaves 2–4½ in (5–11.5 cm) long

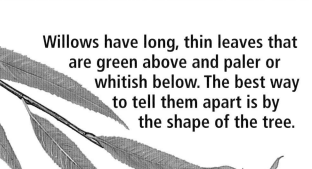

Willows have long, thin leaves that are green above and paler or whitish below. The best way to tell them apart is by the shape of the tree.

Coastal Plain Willow

(Salix caroliniana)

This small tree often grows only as a shrub. Its branches spread or slightly droop. It grows alongside streams and swamps across the Coastal Plain. The leaves are very hairy when they first open.
Native to the southeastern U.S.
Grows up to 30 ft (9 m) tall
Leaves 2–4 in (5–10 cm) long

Black Willow

(Salix nigra)

This willow grows very large and has two or three blackish trunks and upright branches. Willows grow in wet soil and are often planted alongside streams and rivers to stop the banks from eroding and thereby prevent flooding. Like other willows, the flowers are long, yellow or green catkins. The wood is used for furniture, doors, toys, and boxes.
Native to the eastern and southern U.S.
Grows up to 100 ft (30 m) tall
Leaves 3–5 in (7.5–12.5 cm) long

Babylon Weeping Willow

(Salix babylonica)

This weeping willow is planted in parks, gardens, and cemeteries, especially near water. New twigs are yellowish-green and hang straight down. By winter they have turned olive-brown. It is one of the first willows to come into leaf and among the last to shed its leaves.
Introduced from China Planted on East Coast and west to Missouri in the U.S.
Grows up to 40 ft (12 m) tall
Leaves 2½–5 in (6.5–12.5 cm) long

Peachleaf Willow

(Salix amygdaloides)

The peachleaf willow is smaller than the black willow, and its leaves are shorter and wider. It is planted along riverbanks to prevent erosion.
Native to southern Canada and the northern U.S.
Grows up to 60 ft (18 m) tall
Leaves 2–4½ in (5–11.5 cm) long

Oaks

The best way to recognize an oak tree is by its acorns and leaves. There are several groups of oaks. White oaks have deeply lobed leaves. Some types of red oaks have pointed and deeply lobed leaves. The leaves of willow oaks and live oaks have few or no lobes.

Post Oak
(Quercus stellata)

The best way to identify a post oak is from its leaves. The two middle lobes are larger than the rest, so the whole leaf is shaped something like a cross. As its name suggests, the wood is used for posts and also for railroad ties and in building construction.
Native to the southern and eastern U.S.
Grows up to 100 ft (30 m) tall
Leaves 3–6 in (7.5–15 cm) long

Bur Oak
(Quercus macrocarpa)

This white oak gets its name from the hairy, scaly cup which holds its acorns—up to 2 inches (5 centimeters) long, longer than any other native oak. The leaves are also extremely large.
Native to southern Canada, the American Midwest, and south to Texas
Grows up to 80 ft (24 m) tall
Leaves 4–10 in (10–25.5 cm) long

Pin Oak
(Quercus palustris)

Pin oaks are a very common shade tree along many city streets in the East and West. You can tell a pin oak from its slender, pinlike twigs and the tufts of hairs on the undersides of the shiny, dark green leaves. Look too at the acorns. They are nearly round and held in a thin, saucer-shaped cup.
Native from the Midwest to East Coast of the U.S.
Grows up to 90 ft (27 m) tall
Leaves 3–5 in (7.5–12.5 cm) long

White Oak
(Quercus alba)

This tree is the most common member of the white oak group. The leaves are bright green above and whitish below. They turn red or brown in fall and often remain on the tree. Look for the dangling, male catkins in spring. The female flowers develop into acorns, which provide food for birds, squirrels, and other animals. The acorn cup is very shallow. White oaks have sturdy trunks and wide, spreading branches. The colonists used them for building ships. Their wood is still important and is used for making barrels for whiskey.
Native to southeastern Canada and the eastern U.S.
Grows up to 100 ft (30 m) tall
Leaves 4–9 in (10–23 cm) long

Willow Oak
(Quercus phellos)

This tree gets its name from its leaves, which look something like those of a willow tree (see page 15). The leaves turn from green to pale yellow in fall. The slender branches give plenty of shade. Animals feed on the acorns.

Native to the southern U.S. and north, along the East Coast to New Jersey
Grows up to 80 ft (24 m) tall
Leaves 2–4½ in (5–11.5 cm) long

Red Oak
(Quercus rubra)

Red oaks are named for the color of their leaves in autumn. Although these leaves are dull green in spring and summer, they turn dark red or brown in fall. Acorns remain on red oaks at all times. The acorns are small and take two years to develop. The tree has stout, spreading branches. The wood is strong and is used for furniture and flooring.

Native to southern Canada and the eastern U.S.
Grows up to 90 ft (27 m) tall
Leaves 4–9 in (10–23 cm) long

Chestnut Oak
(Quercus prinus)

Chestnut oaks get their name from their leaves, which look something like those of the American chestnut (see page 21). They have wavy or toothed edges, rather than lobed. The acorns are a shiny dark brown. The gray bark becomes thick and ridged and is full of tannin.

Native to New England and the eastern U.S.
Grows up to 80 ft (24 m) tall
Leaves 4–8 in (10–20 cm) long

Live Oak
(Quercus virginiana)

Live oaks are trees in the red oak group that are evergreen. The thick, oval leaves sometimes have a pointed tip. Live oaks usually grow in sandy soils, including dunes and marshes. Clumps of Spanish moss often hang from them. A slightly different variety with smaller leaves grows in the United States in Texas.

Native to the Gulf Coast and East Coast of the U.S. as far north as Virginia
Grows up to 50 ft (15 m) tall Leaves 1½–4 in (4–10 cm) long

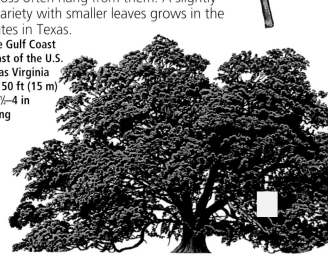

How a Tree Grows

Trees never stop growing. Every year new shoots grow at the ends of the branches making the crown wider and taller. And every year a new layer of wood forms under the bark, making the trunk and branches a little thicker.

Estimating a tree's height

1 **Take 29 equal paces away from the tree.** Ask a friend to hold a stick upright at that point.
2 **Walk another pace away from the tree.** Crouch or lie down so that your eye is as low as the ground.
3 **Look past the stick to the top of the tree.** Ask your friend to raise or lower his or her hand on the stick until the bottom of the hand lines up with the tree's top.
4 **Measure the distance from your friend's hand to the ground** in inches, and multiply this number by 30.
5 **Divide this answer by 12,** and you will have the rough height of the tree in feet.

Inside a tree's trunk

When a tree has been blown over or chopped down, take a look at the pattern of rings in the stump. They can tell you the whole history of the tree, because each ring represents the layer of wood formed in one year of the tree's life.

1 **Count the rings to find out how old the tree was.**
2 **Look for rings which are particularly wide or narrow.** Wide rings show years when the tree had plenty of rain and grew well. Narrow rings show years of drought (little rain) or cold weather when the tree grew only a little.
3 **If the rings are closer together on one side than the other,** try to work out why the tree grew less on the crowded side. Is there a wall or another tree close by?

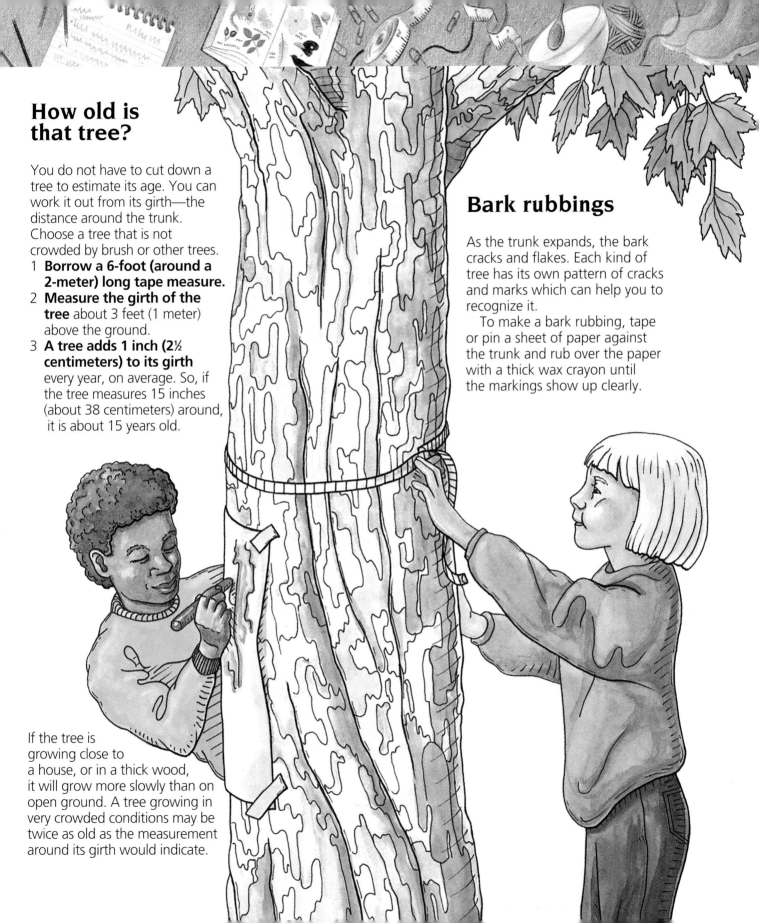

How old is that tree?

You do not have to cut down a tree to estimate its age. You can work it out from its girth—the distance around the trunk. Choose a tree that is not crowded by brush or other trees.

1 **Borrow a 6-foot (around a 2-meter) long tape measure.**
2 **Measure the girth of the tree** about 3 feet (1 meter) above the ground.
3 **A tree adds 1 inch (2½ centimeters) to its girth** every year, on average. So, if the tree measures 15 inches (about 38 centimeters) around, it is about 15 years old.

If the tree is growing close to a house, or in a thick wood, it will grow more slowly than on open ground. A tree growing in very crowded conditions may be twice as old as the measurement around its girth would indicate.

Bark rubbings

As the trunk expands, the bark cracks and flakes. Each kind of tree has its own pattern of cracks and marks which can help you to recognize it.

To make a bark rubbing, tape or pin a sheet of paper against the trunk and rub over the paper with a thick wax crayon until the markings show up clearly.

Hawthorns & Sycamores

You can tell hawthorns by their jagged, toothed, or lobed leaves and spiky thorns.

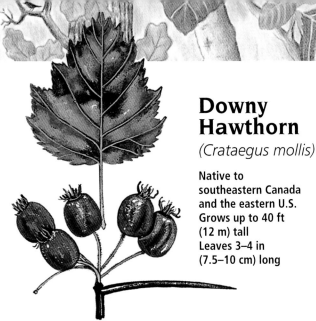

Downy Hawthorn
(Crataegus mollis)

Native to southeastern Canada and the eastern U.S.
Grows up to 40 ft (12 m) tall
Leaves 3–4 in (7.5–10 cm) long

Washington Hawthorn
(Crataegus phaenopyrum)

This is one of the showiest and most attractive hawthorns, and it is often planted in cities in the East. It flowers in late spring. In fall the leaves turn scarlet and orange before dropping. The shiny red berries, called haws, stay on the tree all winter.

Native to the eastern U.S.
Grows up to 30 ft (9 m) tall
Leaves 1½–2½ in (4–6.5 cm) long

The young leaves of downy hawthorn are covered with white hair, as are the young twigs and fruits. The flowers are larger than other hawthorns and grow into drooping clusters of dark red berries with dark spots. Some downy hawthorns have thorns up to 2½ inches (6.5 centimeters) long, while others have almost no thorns at all.

Scarlet Hawthorn
(Crataegus coccinea)

You cannot miss hawthorns in the spring when they are covered with white flowers. Scarlet hawthorn grows into a small, sturdy tree and is named for its red berries. They have many dark spots on them. Black hawthorn has similar leaves but black berries. It grows mainly in the West.

Native from Iowa and Minnesota east to the Canadian and U.S. coasts
Grows up to 20 ft (6 m) tall
Leaves 2–4 in (5–10 cm) long

Sycamores and London planes have large leaves with five lobes, rather like the five fingers of a hand. Chestnuts have long, narrow, toothed leaves.

Sycamore
(Platanus occidentalis)

Sycamores can grow to be very tall and have large, straight trunks. Some trunks measure more than 10 feet (3 meters) across. The bark is blue-white and peels off the trunk in large flakes, leaving brown, gray, and green patches. On very large trunks, the bark is dark brown and furrowed into deep, scaly ridges. The tiny green flowers turn into brown balls, which hang down individually on long stalks.
Native to the eastern U.S.
Grows up to 175 ft (53 m) tall
Leaves 4–8 in (10–20 cm) long

London Plane
(Platanus x acerifolia)

This tree has been planted in cities from coast to coast in the United States. It stands up well to pollution and to having its roots below concrete. It can be distinguished from an American sycamore as its leaves have deeper lobes.
Hybrid between sycamore and Oriental plane
Planted across the U.S. and U.K.
Up to 100 ft (30 m) tall
Leaves 5–10 in (12.5–25.5 cm) long

American Chestnut
(Castanea dentata)

An American chestnut can be recognized by its long, toothed leaves and from its fruit. Look for the spiny burs that split open to release two or three shiny brown chestnuts. American chestnuts are often more like shrubs than trees. They have been virtually wiped out in many parts of the United States by chestnut blight. Hybrids of Chinese and American trees, however, resist the disease and are being developed to replace the original species.
Native to the eastern and southeastern U.S.
Grows up to 20 ft (6 m) tall, formerly up to 70 ft (21 m)
Leaves 5–9 in (12.5–23) long

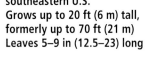

Maples

All maples have pairs of leaves, mostly with 3- or 5-pointed lobes. The middle lobe is sometimes divided again into more lobes.

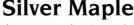

Silver Maple
(Acer saccharinum)

Silver maples get their name from the silvery underside of their leaves. When the wind blows, the leaves seem to turn silver. Even when the leaves turn yellow or red in fall, the underside remains silver. The smooth bark is silvery-gray. Clusters of deep red flowers open in early spring before the leaves. Pairs of winged seeds form in early summer and are scattered by the wind.

**Native across the eastern U.S. and southeastern Canada
Grows up to 80 ft (24 m) tall—Leaves 4–6 in (10–15 cm) long**

Sugar Maple
(Acer saccharum)

The leaves of the sugar maple turn brilliant reds, oranges, and yellows in fall. This tree can be distinguished from silver maple by its more rounded, tapering form. The wood is used for furniture, flooring, and boxes, and also as a thin layer, or veneer, over other woods. Each tree can give up to 60 gallons (227 liters) of sap each year. This can be made into maple sugar and syrup.

Native across eastern North America, but not the southeastern U.S. Grows up to 135 ft (41 m) tall Leaves 3½–5½ in (9–14 cm) long

Red Maple
(Acer rubrum)

In fall, the red maple has red seeds and autumn leaves. In spring, look for its red flowers and shoots. The underside of the leaves is silvery, like the silver maple, but the leaves are smaller and less deeply lobed. The leaf of the red maple is Canada's national emblem.

Native in southeastern Canada and across the eastern and Midwestern U.S. Grows up to 90 ft (27 m) tall Leaves 2½–4 in (6.5–10 cm) long

Boxelder
(Acer negundo)

Although boxelder is a maple, its compound leaves are more like those of an ash. Its pairs of winged seeds place it in the maple family, however. Many of these seeds hang on the tree right through winter. Boxelders grow by roadsides, as well as along streams and in moist valleys.

Native throughout the U.S. and Canada Grows up to 60 ft (18 m) tall Leaves 6 in (15 cm) long

Rocky Mountain Maple
(Acer glabrum)

This low, bushy tree is the common small maple of the Western mountains.

Native to the Rocky Mountains from Alaska to New Mexico
Grows up to 30 ft (9 m) tall
Leaves 1½–4½ in (4–11.5 cm) long

Sycamore Maple
(Acer pseudoplatanus)

Also called the planetree maple, this tree grows well in poor soils and polluted cities. The leaves, however, are not as spectacular in fall as many of the maples native to North America.
Introduced from Europe—Planted across the U.S.
Grows up to 70 ft (21 m) tall
Leaves 3½–6 in (9–15 cm) long

Norway Maple
(Acer platanoides)

This tree is similar to the sugar maple, and they are often planted together along streets. The leaves of the Norway maple are generally longer and wider than those of the sugar maple. The tree is at its best in spring, when the yellow flowers open before the leaves, and in fall, when the leaves turn deep yellow.

Introduced from northern and central Europe
Planted across the U.S. and southern Canada
Grows up to 90 ft (27 m) tall
Leaves 4–7 in (10–18 cm) long

Buckeyes & Ashes

Buckeyes and horsechestnuts have large, palmate, or hand-shaped, leaves with five to seven leaflets.

Horsechestnut
(Aesculus hippocastanum)

Horsechestnut, also called European horsechestnut, is a noticeable tree in spring when it is covered with big, white, candle-shaped flowers. By fall, the flowers have turned into shiny brown nuts in spiky cases. Unlike sweet chestnuts, the nuts of the horsechestnut are poisonous. It was said that long ago in Turkey, the nuts were used to make a cough medicine for horses, and so the tree got its name.
Introduced from southeastern Europe
Widely planted in streets and parks
across the U.S. and southern Canada
Grows up to 70 ft (21 m) tall
Leaves 3–7 in (7.5–18 cm) long

Yellow Buckeye
(Aesculus flava)

Buckeyes can be distinguished from horsechestnuts by looking at the trees' leaves. Horsechestnut leaflets have no stalks of their own, while buckeye leaflets join at the end of short stalks. In fall, the leaves turn brilliant orange or yellow. The flowers are yellow and the nuts are held in a smooth, or slightly pitted, case.
Native to the
central U.S.
Grows up to
90 ft (27 m) tall
Leaves 3½–7 in
(9–18 cm) long

Ohio Buckeye
(Aesculus glabra)

This is the state tree of Ohio. It can be differentiated from other buckeyes by crushing one of the leaves or twigs. If it smells unpleasant, then it is Ohio buckeye. The nuts are held in spiny cases.
Native from Pennsylvania
to Oklahoma and in the
Canadian Prairie Provinces
Grows up to 70 ft
(21 m) tall
Leaves 2–6 in
(5–15 cm) long

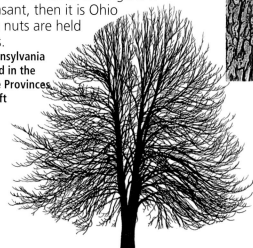

You can recognize ash trees by their leaves, which are divided into many pairs of leaflets with a single leaflet at the tip, and by the bunches of long-winged seeds.

Black Ash
(Fraxinus nigra)

Black ash grows mainly in the northeast in wet, swampy soils and in forests of coniferous and broadleaf trees. The soft, scaly plates of its gray bark rub off easily. The tree gets its name from the dark brown inner wood, or heartwood. Black ash wood is split into strips and made into baskets and barrel hoops. Not surprisingly, it is also known as the basket ash and the hoop ash.
Native to eastern Canada and the northeastern U.S.
Grows up to 50 ft (15 m) tall
Leaves 12–16 in (30–40 cm) long

Native to southern Canada and the U.S. east of the Rocky Mountains
Grows up to 60 ft (18 m) tall in northern areas
Leaves 6–10 in (15–25.5 cm) long

Red Ash
(Fraxinus pennsylvanica)

Red ash, also known as green ash, is the most widespread ash tree. You can recognize the red ash by its leaves. Leaves of red ash are shiny green above, and paler and slightly hairy beneath, while those of the white ash are dark green above, and whitish and sometimes hairy below. The flowers are greenish and have no petals.

White Ash
(Fraxinus americana)

White ash is a very common Eastern ash. It grows wild in upland areas with other broadleaf trees and conifers. The purple flowers do not have any petals. Look for the flowers in spring before the leaves come out. Male and female flowers grow on separate trees. In fall the clusters of long-winged seeds hang from the female trees. The wood of white ash is used for making baseball bats, oars, hockey sticks, and other sports equipment.
Native to eastern North America
Grows up to 80 ft (24 m) tall
Leaves 8–12 in (20–30 cm) long

Oregon Ash
(Fraxinus latifolia)

This Western ash prefers the wet soils of stream banks. It has very large leaves on hairy shoots.
Native to the West Coast of the U.S.
Grows up to 80 ft (24 m) tall
Leaves 5–12 in (12.5–30 cm) long

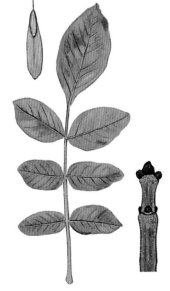

Walnuts & Hickories

Hickories belong to the walnut family. Their leaves have many paired leaflets, like those of ash trees. You can tell them from ash trees because they produce nuts, rather than winged seeds.

Pecan

(Carya illinoensis)

Pecans have great economic value, especially for their edible nuts. These oblong nuts are covered with a thin, brown shell. The wood of the tree is also valuable and is used for furniture, flooring, and paneling.
Native to the Mississippi Valley
Planted across the eastern U.S.
and commercially in the southern U.S.
Grows up to 180 ft (50 m) tall
Leaves 12–20 in
(30–50 cm) long

Black Walnut

(Juglans nigra)

The black walnut has long leaves with numerous leaflets that are spaced evenly apart. The bark is dark brown with deep, scaly ridges. The wood is valuable for making furniture and gunstocks. The nuts are hidden inside hard, thick shells with thick, green, outer husks. The nuts must be picked early, however, because squirrels and other animals like to eat them.
Native to the eastern U.S.
Grows up to 90 ft (27 m) tall
Leaves 12–24 in (30–60 cm) long

Bitternut Hickory

(Carya cordiformis)

This is the most common and widely distributed hickory. It can be recognized by its small, bright yellow buds in winter. The nuts are much too bitter even for animals to eat, although a few rabbits have been seen to nibble them.
Native to the northern
and eastern U.S.
and eastern Canada
Grows up to 80 ft (24 m) tall
Leaves 6–10 in (15–25.5 cm) long

Shagbark Hickory
(Carya ovata)

This tree is named after its rough, shaggy bark, which flakes into long, curly strips. The bark of shellbark hickory is similar, but a shellbark leaf has seven leaflets, rather than five. The name *hickory* comes from the Native American word *pawcohiccora*—which was the oily food the Native Americans made after soaking the nuts in boiling water.

Native to the eastern U.S. and southeastern Canada
Grows up to 100 ft (30 m) tall
Leaves 8–14 in (20–35 cm) long

Mockernut Hickory
(Carya tomentosa)

A leaf of mockernut hickory has seven or nine leaflets. It can be recognized by the strong smell emitted when a leaf is crushed, and by the dense hairs that cover the undersides of the leaves. The round nuts are edible but must be collected early, before they are gathered by squirrels and other animals. Hickory wood is used for furniture, flooring, baseball bats, and skis.

Native to the eastern U.S.
Grows up to 80 ft (24 m) tall
Leaves 8–20 in (20–50 cm) long

Pignut Hickory
(Carya glabra)

Sometimes called smoothbark hickory, after its smooth, light gray bark, this is one of the most common hickories in the southern Appalachians of the United States. Each of its leaves usually has only five leaflets, and its nuts open later than those of other trees. The nuts may be sweet or bitter.

Native to southeastern Canada and the eastern U.S.
Grows up to 80 ft (24 m) tall
Leaves 6–10 in (15–25.5 cm) long

Other Broadleaf Trees

Hackberry, sugarberry, and Japanese zelkova belong to the elm family. Their toothed, oval leaves end in a long point. You can tell them apart by their fruit.

Sugarberry
(Celtis laevigata)

Sugarberries are hackberries whose berries are orange-red in color. Robins, mockingbirds, and other songbirds feed on them. This tree can grow very tall, and it is used as an ornamental shade tree.
Native to the southeastern U.S.
Grows up to 80 ft (24 m) tall
Leaves 2½–4 in (6.5–10 cm) long

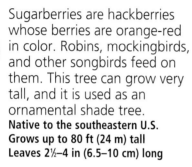

Hackberry
(Celtis occidentalis)

The leaves of hackberries are similar to those of elms (see page 12), but the fruit is quite different. Instead of winged nutlets, hackberries have dark purple berries. Woodpeckers, pheasants, and other birds feed on these sweetish berries. Mites and fungi also like hackberries. They produce the deformed bushy growths in the branches, known as "witches'-brooms."
Native to the Midwest and northeastern U.S., north to Quebec, Canada—Grows up to 50 ft (15 m) tall
Leaves 2–5 in (5–12.5 cm) long

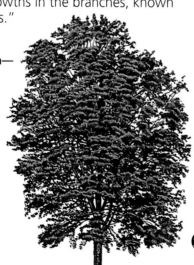

Japanese Zelkova
(Zelkova serrata)

This tree, also known as keaki, is particularly attractive in fall when the green leaves turn yellow, orange, and red. It is resistant to Dutch elm disease and so makes a good substitute for American elms.
Introduced from East Asia
Grows up to 70 ft (21 m) tall
Leaves 1–3½ in (2.5–9 cm) long

Sassafras and sweet gum both have aromatic bark. Ailanthus (tree of heaven), honey locust, and Kentucky coffeetree have many pairs of small leaflets.

Sassafras
(Sassafras albidum)

The leaves of sassafras vary in shape—some are oval, others are shaped like mittens, and some have three lobes. All sassafras have dark blue berries growing on long red stalks. When the Europeans first came to America, they thought the aromatic root bark would cure all diseases and shipped it back to Europe. Today, parts of the sassafras are used to perfume soap and to flavor root beer.
Native to the southern and eastern U.S.
Grows up to 30 ft (10 m) tall
Leaves 3–5 in (7.5–12.5 cm) long

Sweet Gum
(Liquidambar styraciflua)

Sweet gum leaves look rather like maple leaves (see page 22) and, like them, they turn scarlet in fall. But sweet gum gives off a strong, sweet, aromatic smell when a leaf is crushed. The tree has drooping, prickly, brown fruits. Pioneers collected resin from under the bark and used it in medicines and chewing gum.
Native to the eastern and southeastern U.S.
Grows up to 100 ft (30 m) tall
Leaves 3–6 in (7.5–15 cm) long

Kentucky Coffeetree
(Gymnocladus dioicus)

This tree can be identified by its leaves, up to 3 feet (90 centimeters) long, which are made up of many leaflets. Its brown pods each contain several brown seeds that were once used as a substitute for coffee, which was how the tree got its name. The raw seeds, however, are poisonous.
Native to the Midwest—Rare in the wild
Grows up to 100 ft (30 m) tall
Leaves 24–36 in (60–90 cm) long

Ailanthus
(Ailanthus altissima)

Also called tree of heaven, this tree has been planted in nearly every city in North America. The leaves are deep red when they first open, then change to green. They feature two large teeth, or small lobes, near the stalk. The clusters of yellow, male flowers smell unpleasant, and some people are allergic to their pollen.
Introduced from China
Grows across temperate North America
Grows up to 60 ft (18 m) tall
Leaves 12–24 in (30–60 cm) long

Honey Locust
(Gleditsia triacanthos)

The trunks and branches of most wild honey locusts are covered with groups of sharp spines, but a variety without spines is usually planted in urban areas. The tree is a good one for attracting wildlife. They like to feed on the sweet pulp of its long, thin pods.

Native to the Midwest of the U.S., south to Gulf of Mexico
Planted widely in cities
Grows up to 80 ft (24 m) tall
Leaves 4–8 in (10–20 cm) long

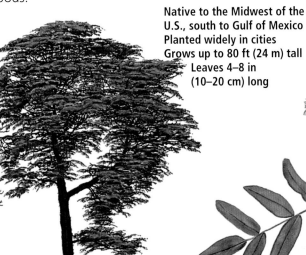

Leaves

Leaves are the tree's food factories. While they are making food for the tree, they give off oxygen, which is part of the air we all breathe. Nearly all living things need oxygen to stay alive.

Leaves are green because they contain a pigment called chlorophyll. This chemical traps the energy of sunlight and allows a plant to use water taken from the soil and carbon dioxide gathered from the air to make sugar. This sugar dissolves in more water to become sap, the tree's food, which is taken down thin tubes (veins) to the roots where it is stored. During this process, called photosynthesis, the tree releases oxygen back into the air.

Leaf skeletons

You can see the veins in a leaf most clearly when the rest of the leaf has gone. Sycamore leaves are good ones to use.

1 **Boil 2 pints (5 cups) of water in a large pan** and add 1 tablespoon of borax (washing soda). Ask an adult to help you with this.
2 **Drop the leaves into the pan** and leave them to simmer for half an hour.
3 **When the pan has cooled**, drain and rinse the leaves in cold water and leave to dry.
4 **Use an old toothbrush** to carefully brush away all of the leaf except the veins.

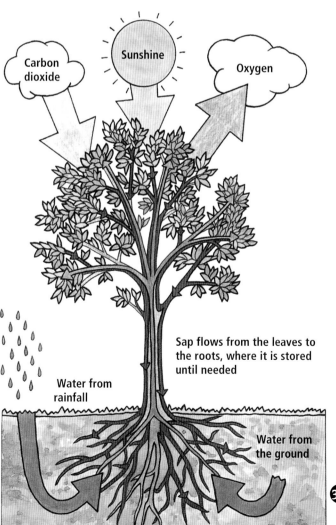

Carbon dioxide

Sunshine

Oxygen

Sap flows from the leaves to the roots, where it is stored until needed

Water from rainfall

Water from the ground

Collecting leaves

A good time to collect leaves is when they have fallen off the trees. Most broadleaf trees drop their leaves every autumn. Once the chlorophyll in a leaf breaks down, the leaf can no longer make sap for the tree. The tiny pipelines that carry water up from the roots to the leaf and sap down from the leaf to the roots become plugged. The tree no longer sends water up to the leaves and they wither and fall off the tree.

1 **Collect as many different leaves as you can.** Arrange them carefully on sheets of paper towel.
2 **Start with four layers of folded newspaper** on a flat, hard surface. Next put a paper towel with leaves on top of it. Add another sheet of paper towel and then newspaper on top of it.
3 **Keep adding layers** until you have a stack about 6 inches (15 centimeters) high. Put some heavy books on top and leave for 2 to 3 weeks until dry.
4 **Glue your leaves on to sheets of paper** to make a picture.

Changing color

The leaves of some trees change from green to fantastic shades of yellow, orange, and brown before they fall. Why do leaves change color?
The green color in leaves comes from chlorophyll, which hides all the other colors. As autumn approaches, the shorter days and cooler nights cause the chlorophyll to break down. As the chlorophyll breaks down, the other colors in the leaves— yellow, orange, and red— appear.

1 **Watch a tree in autumn** whose leaves change color. In what order do the colors appear?
2 **In spring, look for trees** like the Kwanzan cherry (see page 39), whose leaves are bronze-red at first. Watch them turn green as the chlorophyll in them builds up.

Ornamental Trees

Many of the trees planted along streets and in parks and yards have been introduced from countries as far away as Japan, China, and India. These ornamental trees, some of which are quite small, all have been planted because they are particularly decorative in some way.

Although some ornamental trees are fruit trees, of the ornamental trees in this book, only those on pages 34 and 35 produce fruits that can be eaten. The apples and cherries grown on most ornamental trees are too sour for us to eat, though birds, squirrels, and other animals feed on them. These trees are planted for their beautiful blossoms, not their fruits.

Trees such as magnolias are planted for their big, showy flowers. It is easy to recognize them when the flowers are out, but try to spot them at other times of the year as well. Look closely at their leaves, bark, and seeds.

Not all ornamental trees have been introduced from Europe or Asia. Eastern redbud and many other trees are natives.

The picture shows several ornamental trees. How many do you recognize?

Fruit Trees

In the right climate, these trees will all produce fruit that can be eaten.

Red Mulberry
(Morus rubra)

Red mulberry grows wild in woods as well as in yards and on roadsides. The toothed leaves are mainly oval, but on young twigs they may have two or three lobes. By late spring, the long, narrow clusters of flowers have developed into dark purple or red berries. Both people and animals, especially songbirds, like to eat the berries. The bark is brown and scaly. The wood is used for furniture, fence posts, and farm tools.
Native to southeastern Canada and the eastern U.S.
Grows up to 60 ft (18 m) tall
Leaves 4–7 in (10–18 cm) long

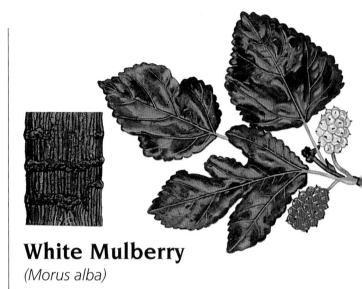

White Mulberry
(Morus alba)

White mulberry can be distinguished from red by its shiny leaves. Leaves of white mulberry are smooth on top, but slightly hairy below. The fruits may be pink, purple, or white. Both birds and people like to eat them. Like other mulberries, they are made up of many tiny, beadlike berries, clustered together. In late spring, the sidewalks are littered with them. In China, the leaves are the main food for silkworms.
Introduced from China—Planted across the U.S. and now grows wild in East and West coast states
Grows up to 40 ft (12 m) tall
Leaves 2½–7 in (6.5–18 cm) long

Fig
(Ficus carica)

Fig trees are easy to recognize from their large, leathery leaves, which are deeply cut into three or five lobes. They are grown for their juicy fruits and may produce two or three crops each year.
Introduced from western Asia
Planted on the West Coast of the U.S.
Grows up to 30 ft (9 m) tall
Leaves up to 12 in (30 cm) long

Common Persimmon
(Diospyros virginiana)

In Arkansas and Oklahoma, persimmons grow in hedges for miles along the road. In other places, persimmon grows in woods and clearings near tall trees. The yellowy-white flowers open in summer and develop into orange or purple-brown berries. They are very tart at first, but when they have fully ripened, they are sweet enough to eat and taste something like dates. Persimmon desserts are a Christmas treat in the southern United States. Opossums, raccoons, skunks, deer, and birds like to eat these berries. The wood is used to make the heads of golf clubs and as a veneer for furniture.

Native to the southeastern U.S.
Grows up to 70 ft (21 m) tall
Leaves 2½–6 in (6.5–15 cm) long

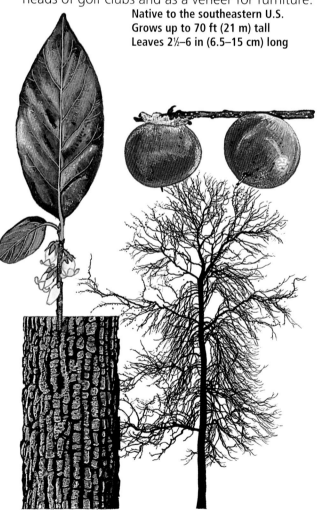

Loquat
(Eriobotyra japonica)

Loquats can only produce fruit in the warmest areas of the United States. The long, toothed leaves stay on the tree all the year round. Loquat grows in courtyards and small gardens. The flowers open in late summer through early winter. In spring, the flowers ripen into round, orange fruits.

Introduced from China and Japan
Grown in California and in southern states in the U.S.
Grows up to 25 ft (7.5 m) tall
Leaves 6–20½ in (15–52 cm) long

Peach
(Prunus persica)

Peach trees are grown, mainly in orchards, for their juicy fruit. But some now grow wild by the side of the road. Peach trees have long, thin leaves and pink flowers that look like pale roses.

Introduced from China
Grown in the Midwest, South, and in California in the U.S.
Grows up to 25 ft (7.5 m) tall
Leaves 3½–6 in (9–15 cm) long

Crab Apples & Pear

These fruit trees are planted because of their attractive blossoms and fruit. Only the sweet crab apple and pear fruits are sweet enough for people to eat.

Pillar Crab Apple
(Malus Tschonoskii)

This tree may be planted in streets and narrow gardens. It does not spread widely and produces only a few small yellow or greenish apples. In fall, the leaves turn brilliant colors. It is also known as the Tschonoski crab.
Introduced from Japan
Grows up to 45 ft (14 m) tall
Leaves up to 5 in (12.5 cm) long

Sweet Crab Apple
(Malus coronaria)

This tree grows wild in moist areas and woods. Crab apples belong to the rose family, and their flowers look like those of wild roses. In parks and gardens, a cultivar called Charlottae, which has double flowers, is often grown. The tiny, yellow-green apples ripen in late summer. They can be made into preserves and cider.
Native from southern Ontario, Canada, into the east, central, and southern U.S.
Grows up to 30 ft (9 m) tall
Leaves 2–4 in (5–10 cm) long

Prairie Crab Apple
(Malus ioensis)

As its name suggests, this tree grows wild alongside streams in the prairies. Birds, squirrels, rabbits, and other animals feed on the small, yellow-green apples. Its flowers are pink and sometimes double. This crab apple is a very popular ornamental species.
Native to the eastern prairies and upper Mississippi Valley of the U.S.
Grows up to 30 ft (9 m) tall
Leaves 2½–4 in (6.5–10 cm) long

Common Pear
(Pyrus communis)

The fruit that grows on this pear tree can be eaten. The white flowers appear in spring. Pear trees live for many years. Their wood is very strong and was used by the French to make dressers and other furniture.

Introduced from Europe and western Asia
Grows wild in the eastern and northwestern U.S.
Grows up to 45 ft (14 m) tall
Leaves 1½–3 in (4–7.5 cm) long

Japanese Crab Apple
(Malus floribunda)

This tree has been planted in many urban gardens. It is at its best in midspring, when both the bright red buds and the pink and white flowers can be seen. The fruits are small and yellow.

Introduced from Japan—Planted in Ontario, Canada, south to Delaware and in California in the U.S.
Grows up to 30 ft (9 m) tall
Leaves 1½–3½ in (4–9 cm) long

Purple Crab Apple
(Malus x purpurea)

The purple crab apple is well named for its purplish flowers. It has dark red fruit no more than 1 inch (2.5 centimeters) long. When the leaves first open, they are purplish-red, but they soon turn green.

Hybrid—Introduced from France
Grows up to 25 ft (7.5 m) tall
Leaves 3–4 in (7.5–10 cm) long

Cherry Trees

The leaves of cherry trees tend to be longer and slightly narrower than those of apple trees. But the best way to tell them apart is by the bark. Cherry trees often have smooth bark with horizontal bands, while apple trees have ridged, scaly bark.

Black Cherry
(Prunus serotina)

Black cherry grows wild or is planted for shade. It is larger than other cherry trees. Its white flowers grow in long spikes, and its dark gray bark becomes ridged and scaly with age. However, if a leaf or part of the bark is crushed, it smells of cherries. The wood is used for furniture, paneling, and toys, and a cough medicine, called wild cherry syrup, is made from the bark. The small, dark, juicy cherries are made into jelly and wine.

Native to southeastern Canada and the eastern U.S.
Grows up to 80 ft (24 m) tall
Leaves 2–5 in (5–12.5 cm) long

Pin Cherry
(Prunus pensylvanica)

This small tree is sometimes called fire cherry, because it often shoots up on land cleared by forest fires. It has shiny red twigs and narrow leaves. The white flowers have long stalks and grow in clusters of three to five. Although the light red cherries taste sour, they make good jelly. The cherries are also eaten by birds and animals.

Native to almost all of Canada and south through the Appalachians to the southern and western U.S.
Grows up to 30 ft (9 m) tall
Leaves 2½–4½ in (6.5–11.5 cm) long

Chokecherry
(Prunus virginiana)

This small tree or shrub grows along streams and roads, on mountains, and in forest clearings. Its leaves are shorter and more oval than those of the black cherry or pin cherry. The shiny, dark red cherries are so sour they can make people choke, which is how the tree got its name. The cherries can, however, be made into jelly. Look for the silvery webs of tent caterpillars among the twigs.

Native to much of Canada and the U.S., except in parts of the South
Grows up to 20 ft (6 m) tall
Leaves 1½–3¼ in (4–8 cm) long

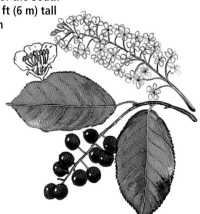

All the cherry trees on this page have been introduced to Canada and the United States. They are planted for their blossoms, not for their fruit.

Pissard Plum
(Prunus cerasidera 'Pissardii')

This is a form of plum tree known as a cherry plum. The buds open up into starry, pale pink flowers that grow singly, not in clusters. The flowers are followed by purple or brownish-red leaves.
Introduced from Iran
Grows up to 33 ft (10 m) tall
Leaves 2½ in (6.5 cm) long

Pink Weeping Cherry
(Prunus subhirtella 'Pendula rubra')

This tree features drooping branches and delicate, pink flowers, which cover it in late March or early April.
Introduced from Japan
Grows up to 40 ft (12 m) tall
Leaves 1–4 in (2.5–10 cm) long

Japanese Cherry "Shirotae"
(Prunus 'Shirotae')

This is the first Japanese cherry to flower in the spring. It has single, white flowers all along its branches.
Introduced from Japan
Grows up to 25 ft (7.5 m) tall
Leaves 4½ in (11.5 cm) long

Japanese Cherry "Kwanzan"
(Prunus 'Kwanzan')

Of Japanese cherries planted in North America, this is probably the most common variety. It has clusters of florid, pink flowers and shiny bark with many horizontal stripes.
Introduced from Japan
Grows up to 40 ft (12 m) tall
Leaves 2½ in (6.5 cm) long

Trees with Pods of Seeds

All of these trees, except the tallowtree, produce pods of seeds, just like peas do. Look at the trees on page 29; they produce pods as well.

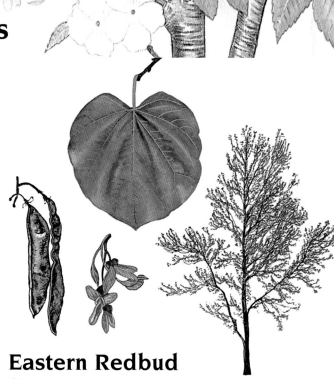

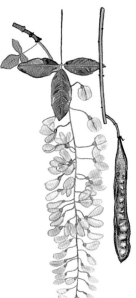

Golden Chain Tree
(Laburnum anagyroides)

This small, yard tree is also known as the common laburnum. It is very noticeable in spring when it is hung with long catkins of yellow flowers. The flowers give way to pods of poisonous, black seeds. The leaves are divided into three oval leaflets.

Native to Europe
Most common in British Columbia, Canada, and in Idaho and Washington in the U.S.
Grows up to 26 ft (7.5 m) tall
Leaves 2½–3½ in (6.5–9 cm) long

Eastern Redbud
(Cercis canadensis)

This small, bushy tree grows wild in woods, but it is also planted along city streets and in gardens. It is at its best in early spring, before the leaves come out, when it is covered with clusters of rose-pink flowers. These flowers can be eaten in salads or fried. They give way to thin, flat pods, which are pink at first, but turn blackish as they ripen. The tree has dull green, heart-shaped leaves.

Native to much of the eastern U.S.
Grows up to 40 ft (12 m) tall
Leaves 2½–4½ in (6.5–11.5 cm) long

Tallowtree
(Sapium sebiferum)

Tallowtree does not produce pods of seeds, but it does have clusters of tiny, yellow-green flowers on stout, 4-inch (10-centimeter) spikes. They can be distinguished from a golden chain tree by their leaves and fruit. The simple leaves are round with a long point. The flowers turn into brown fruits, which split open in fall to show white, waxy seeds. The Chinese used them to make candles.

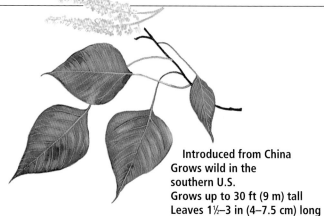

Introduced from China
Grows wild in the southern U.S.
Grows up to 30 ft (9 m) tall
Leaves 1½–3 in (4–7.5 cm) long

Pagoda Tree
(Styphnolobium japonicum)

This tree is also called the Chinese scholar tree and is sometimes planted at universities. Its white flowers do not come out until late summer. The flowers give way to narrow, yellowish pods, which shrink between the seeds so they look like strings of beads. The leaves consist of paired leaflets, which have a strange smell when crushed. The branches twist in the weeping form of the tree. They are called pagoda trees because they are often planted around temples in eastern Asia.

Introduced from China and Korea
Planted across the U.S. in the South
Grows up to 60 ft (18 m) tall
Leaves 6–10 in (15–25.5 cm) long

Silk-tree
(Albizia julibrissin)

This tree can be recognized by its fernlike leaves and pink flowers. The flowers look like balls of long threads. The tree is also called mimosa, because the leaves fold up at night. (The leaves of true mimosa, or sensitive plant, fold up when touched.) The tree has a broad, flat crown.

Introduced from Asia
Planted in the southeastern
U.S. and west to Texas
Grows up to 20 ft (6 m) tall
Leaves 6–15 in (15–38 cm) long

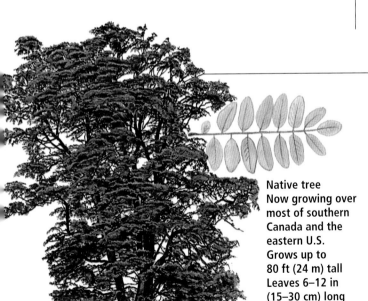

Native tree
Now growing over most of southern Canada and the eastern U.S.
Grows up to 80 ft (24 m) tall
Leaves 6–12 in (15–30 cm) long

Black Locust
(Robinia pseudoacacia)

Black locust trees are most noticeable in late spring when the hanging clusters of white, fragrant flowers are out. These flowers give way to narrow, flat, dark brown pods of beans. The pairs of leaflets fold up at night. Be careful, as the twigs are covered with pairs of short spines. American Indians used the wood to make bows, and the first colonists used it for the corner posts of their houses.

Magnolias & Others

Magnolias have large, spectacular flowers. Both the leaves and the flowers help to tell them apart. Southern catalpa and royal paulownia also have attractive flowers.

Cucumber Tree
(Magnolia acuminata)

Cucumber tree belongs to the magnolia family, but is named for the shape of its fruit. It has bell-shaped flowers with greenish-yellow or bright yellow petals. They are about 3 inches (7.5 centimeters) wide and turn into dark red, cucumber-shaped fruits, about 3 inches (7.5 centimeters) long. The oval leaves end in a short point and sometimes have wavy edges.

Native to southeastern Canada and the eastern and southern U.S.
Grows up to 80 ft (24 m) tall
Leaves 5–10 in (12.5–25.5 cm) long

Sweetbay
(Magnolia virginiana)

This magnolia tree, also known as swamp magnolia, grows in coastal swamps and beside ponds and rivers. In fall it has red, conelike fruits. The leaves emit a spicy smell when crushed. Although sweetbay loses its leaves in northern winters, it is almost evergreen in the South.

Native to the Gulf and East coasts of the U.S.
Grows up to 60 ft (18 m) tall
Leaves 3–6 in (7.5–15 cm) long

Southern Magnolia
(Magnolia grandiflora)

Southern magnolia has very large, white flowers. They may be up to 9 inches (23 centimeters) across. The thick evergreen leaves turn under slightly at the edges. They are shiny, bright green above, but are covered with orange-brown hairs below.

Native in the far South of the U.S.
Planted farther north to North Carolina
Grows up to 80 ft (24 m) tall
Leaves 5–8 in (12.5–20 cm) long

Saucer Magnolia
(Magnolia soulangiana)

Saucer magnolia is the most common yard magnolia. Its large flowers may be pink, purple, or white. Look for the red seeds in early fall, when the long, conelike fruits split open. These magnolias can be distinguished from native varieties because they flower before their leaves open, and the flowers open to a broad, saucerlike shape.

Hybrid of the Chinese trees
Planted widely across the U.S.
Grows up to 25 ft (7.5 m) tall
Leaves 5–8 in (12.5–20 cm) long

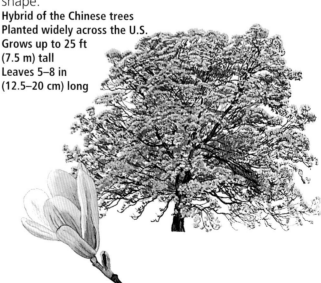

Royal Paulownia

(Paulownia tomentosa)

This fast-growing tree adapts to roadsides and
other areas where it has not been planted. It is
sometimes confused with catalpa. Royal paulownia
has enormous leaves and pale violet, bell-shaped
flowers. The hairy, brown flower buds form in late
summer and are very visible in winter. The flowers
are followed by egg-shaped seed capsules. As they
ripen, the capsules turn from green to brown.
They split open to release the winged seeds.
Introduced from China
Now grows wild in the eastern and southern U.S.
Grows up to 50 ft (15 m) tall
Leaves 6–16 in (15–40 cm) long

Southern Catalpa

(Catalpa bignonioides)

Southern catalpa has large,
heart-shaped leaves, which
smell unpleasant when
crushed. They feature clusters
of white flowers in mid-summer.
Each bell-shaped flower has
two orange stripes and many
purple spots and stripes.
They turn into long, narrow,
cigar-shaped pods, which stay
on the tree during the winter.
When they split in two in
winter, brown seeds with
papery wings are released.

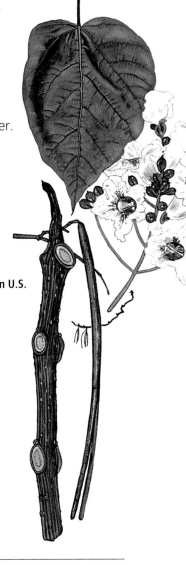

Native to the southern U.S.
Planted in parks and
gardens in Canada
and the U.S.
Grows up to 50 ft
(15 m) tall
Leaves 5–10 in
(12.5–25.5 cm) long

Umbrella Magnolia

(Magnolia tripetala)

This tree can be recognized by its very
long leaves and large, white flowers.
The spreading leaves are said to look
like the ribs of an umbrella. The
flowers have an unpleasant smell.
Their three green sepals are
longer than the petals.

Native to
mountain valleys
and forests in
the eastern U.S.
Grows up to
40 ft (12 m) tall
Leaves 10–20 in
(25.5–51 cm) long

Other Ornamental Trees

The trees on this page are planted for their attractive flowers, fruits, or fall colors.

Black Tupelo
(Nyssa sylvatica)

Black tupelo can be recognized by its shiny, oval, green leaves, which turn bright red in fall, and from its shape. The tree is tall with many slender, horizontal branches. The greenish flowers develop into small blue-black fruits. They are sour but juicy, and many birds and animals love them.

Native to southeastern Canada and the eastern and southern U.S.
Grows up to 80 ft (24 m) tall
Leaves 2–5 in (5–12.5 cm) long

Golden Raintree
(Koelreuteria paniculata)

Golden raintree has big leaves, made up of toothed leaflets. The yellow flowers turn into yellow or pinkish seed pods, which are hollow except for three black seeds. The Formosan golden raintree is more common in the southern United States. Its seed pods are rose or coral in color.

Introduced from eastern Asia
Planted in parks and squares in the eastern U.S. and on the West Coast
Grows up to 30 ft (9 m) tall
Leaves 6–18 in (15–45.5 cm) long

Crapemyrtle
(Lagerstroemia indica)

Crapemyrtle, with its bright pink or white flowers, only grows in places with long, hot summers. In the fall, the tree shows brown seed capsules containing many seeds. The tree's bark is pale brown and gray and is very smooth.

Introduced from China and nearby areas
Planted around the Gulf Coast in the U.S.
Grows up to 20 ft (6 m) tall
Leaves 1–2 in (2.5–5 cm) long

Flowering Dogwood
(Cornus florida)

This tree is spectacular in spring and fall. It has a spring flower with white "petals," at the center of which is a cluster of tiny, yellow-green flowers each with its own true petals. By fall, the tiny flowers have developed into clusters of shiny, red berries and the leaves have turned red below. The rough bark is reddish-brown. American Indians used it in a cure for malaria.

Native to southeastern Canada and the eastern U.S.
Grows up to 40 ft (12 m) tall
Leaves 2½–5 in (6.5–12.5 cm) long

The trees on this page are similar to the elms and ashes shown on pages 12 and 25. These trees, however, are often planted in yards for shade or ornament.

American Mountain Ash
(Sorbus americana)

This small tree has clusters of white flowers in spring, followed by red berries in fall. Cedar waxwings and grouse feed on the berries. Moose prefer to eat the leaves and winter twigs. The glossy, sticky buds emerge in winter and are red on top and green underneath. The buds open up into leaves with many pairs of toothed leaflets.

Native to northeastern North America from Newfoundland to the Appalachians
Grows up to 30 ft (9 m) tall
Leaves 6–8 in (15–20 cm) long

Siberian Elm
(Ulmus pumila)

Siberian elms grow well in dry places. They grow quickly and can tolerate both heat and cold, as well as poor soils. The tree is sometimes confused with Chinese elm. Siberian elm, however, flowers in early spring and produces rounder seeds than the Chinese variety. The best way to tell them apart is by the bark—Siberian elm has rough, gray or brown bark with furrows.

Introduced from Asia
Grows wild on the plains of the U.S. but planted elsewhere too
Grows up to 60 ft (18 m) tall
Leaves ¾–2 in (2–5 cm) long

Chinese Elm
(Ulmus parvifolia)

The most unusual thing about this tree is that it produces its small, greenish flowers in fall. These flowers form at the base of the leaves. They quickly change into oval seeds held in a pale yellow, oval wing. The dark green leaves are oval, too. They are shiny on top with teeth like a saw around the edge. Perhaps the most attractive part of the tree is its bark. It is pale blue-grey, mottled with brown, and flakes off to show the inner red bark beneath.

Introduced from China, Korea, and Japan
Planted across the U.S., particularly around Gulf of Mexico and on the West Coast
Grows up to 50 ft (15 m) tall
Leaves ¾–2 in (2–5 cm) long

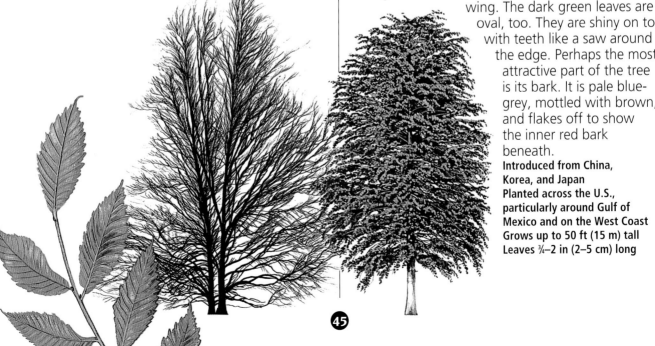

From Flower To Seed

Of the trees that flower, some have male flowers and others female flowers. The male flowers produce millions of grains of pollen, which are blown in the wind or carried by insects to the female flowers on another tree. Some trees have both male and female flowers on the same tree; other trees have flowers that contain both male and female parts. When the right kind of pollen lands on the sticky stigma of the female flower, the pollen grain grows a tube down to the flower's ovary, where it joins with a female egg to produce a seed.

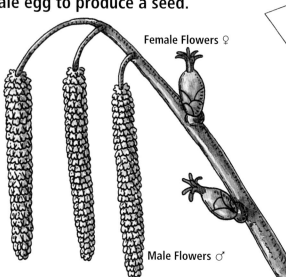

Female Flowers ♀

Male Flowers ♂

Scattering seeds

Most ripe seeds fall on to the ground underneath the tree, but they have a better chance of growing if they are scattered away from the parent tree. For example, berries contain seeds, and animals eat those berries and drop the seeds far from the trees. Or, squirrels and mice may bury stores of nuts (that contain seeds) in the ground to eat during the winter, but some nuts survive to grow into new trees. Trees have a number of other strategies for dispersing seeds away from the parent tree.

Make a winged seed

1 **Copy this shape** on to a piece of paper.
2 **Cut down the center line and fold** one wing one way and the other the opposite way.
3 **Pin a paper clip on to the other end.**

Looking for flowers

All trees have flowers or other structures as a place to make seeds. Some flowers are small and hard to spot, and some are not colored or shaped as you might expect. Look out for the different kinds of flowers.

4 **With an adult's help, stand on a chair** and let the shape go. What happens? Does it always twist the same way?

5 **Experiment** with longer and shorter wings, with two or more paper clips, with wider and narrower stems. Which design flies best?

Black cherry has bright, sweet-smelling flowers to attract insects

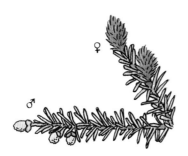
Silver fir has upright female cone flowers and smaller male cone flowers under the branches.

London plane has round female flowers and clusters of yellow male flowers on the same tree.

Seed-bearing structures

The seeds of many trees are enclosed in seed-bearing structures that you can collect—for example, berries from mountain ash, cherry, and hawthorn; nuts from chestnut, beech, oak, hickory, walnut, and others; winged seeds from sycamore, maple, gray birch, and elm. London planes produce round, spiky fruits, while golden chaintrees, black locust, and eastern redbuds produce pods of seeds. All the conifers produce woody cones of seeds.

Mountain ash berries

Beech nut

Winged sycamore seed

Horsechestnut conker

Redbud pod

Woody pine cone

Evergreens & Conifers

The trees described on the first six pages of this section are evergreen broadleaf trees. Unlike the trees in the earlier sections, these do not lose their leaves in winter. All of the conifers, except for those on page 65, are also evergreen. Conifers may be identified by their leaves. Generally, the leaves are thin and sharp, like needles, or cling to the branch like scales.

Most of the trees in the western United States and in northern Canada are conifers. They are in the South too, along with palms and eucalyptus trees. Evergreens can survive very cold and very hot weather better than deciduous trees. Broadleaf evergreens often have leathery, shiny leaves that resist drying out.

Conifer needles have very little surface area, so they do not lose much water. Conifers belong to an ancient, primitive group of plants that evolved before the flowering plants. Some conifers form their seeds very slowly, taking many years. While these seeds develop they are often protected inside a cone. The shape and size of a cone can help to identify a tree.

The conifer trees on pages 58–77 have been arranged according to their fruits and leaves. Those at the beginning do not have cones. They are followed by trees with scaly leaves, and then by trees with single needles. The last trees to be shown are the pines, which have bundles of long, thin needles. The picture shows many types of evergreens. Are there any that you recognize?

Holly & Others

Hollies can be easily recognized by their shiny, prickly leaves. The berries on holly may look beautiful, but they are poisonous. Don't put them in your mouth.

English Holly
(Ilex aquifolium)

English holly has smaller, shinier leaves than American holly. There are many varieties of English holly, and the leaves of these varieties differ in color and shape.
Introduced from southern Europe, north Africa, and west Asia
Planted across the U.S., mainly in states near the coasts
Grows up to 50 ft (15 m) tall
Leaves 1¼–2¾ in (3–7 cm) long

Possumhaw
(Ilex decidua)

Possumhaw is most noticeable in winter, when its gray twigs are covered with small, red berries. Opossums, raccoons, songbirds, and other animals feed on the berries. This tree is a member of the holly family. Its leaves are toothed rather than spiny, and it drops most of them in fall, unlike most other hollies.
Native to the southeastern U.S.
Grows up to 20 ft (6 m) tall
Leaves 1–3 in (2.5–7.5 cm) long

American Holly
(Ilex opaca)

American holly is a narrow tree; it is sometimes clipped into hedges. The leaves are leathery—dark green above and yellow-green below. The tree has clusters of small, white flowers in spring. Male and female flowers grow on separate trees, so only female trees produce the bright red berries. People use the berry-covered branches to decorate their homes at Christmas. Songbirds, game birds, and other animals feed on the bitter-tasting berries.
Native to the southeastern U.S.
and north to Massachusetts
Grows up to 50 ft (15 m) tall
Leaves 2–4 in (5–10 cm) long

Box
(Buxus sempervirens)

Box, or boxwood, can grow as a tree, but it is more common as a shrub or growing as a hedge. It is a good plant for topiary, so you may see it clipped into various ornamental shapes. The tree has small, yellow flowers in spring, which are followed by brown, woody capsules, each containing seeds.

Introduced from Europe
Planted in parks and around public buildings
Grows up to 25 ft (7.5 m) tall
Leaves 1½ in (4 cm) long

Tanoak
(Lithocarpus densiflorus)

Tanoaks are evergreen, as are golden chinquapins, but their leaves have toothed edges and they produce acorns, not spiky seed capsules.
Native to the West Coast of the U.S.
Grows up to 80 ft (24 m) tall
Leaves 2½–5 in (6.5–12.5 cm) long

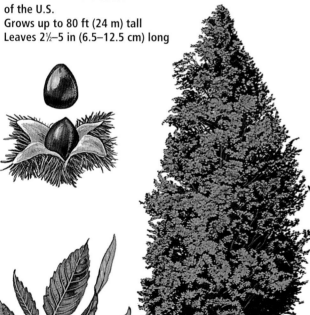

Golden Chinquapin
(Chrysolepis chrysophylla)

Golden chinquapin is similar to American chestnut (see page 21). The long, yellow catkins are mostly male and appear in midsummer. The fruit is a rough bur which matures in autumn of the following year. The leaves are long and oval, but do not have a toothed edge like the American chestnut. They are shiny, dark green above and golden below.
Native to southeast to Oklahoma in the U.S.
Grows up to 80 ft (24 m) tall
Leaves 2–5 in (5–12.5 cm) long

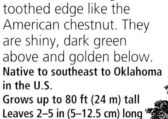

Eucalyptus & Others

Eucalyptus and Russian olives usually have long, thin leaves.

Blue Gum Eucalyptus
(Eucalyptus globulus)

Eucalyptus trees can be recognized by the spicy smell they give off when their long leaves are crushed. The blue gum variety has big blue-white seed capsules and light brown bark, which peels off in long strips, leaving smooth, blue-gray bark below. The young leaves are nearly round and grow in pairs, although the adult leaves are long and narrow. The flowers have no petals, just white or yellow stamens. A "lid" covers them until they make it pop off. The seed capsules often cover the ground beneath the tree.

Introduced from Australia
Now grows wild along the West Coast of the U.S.
Grows up to 120 ft (36.5 m) tall
Leaves 4–12 in (10–30 cm) long

White Iron Bark Eucalyptus
(Eucalyptus leucoxylon)

The medium-sized tree has white or gray bark and lance-shaped leaves. The white iron bark produces clusters of flowers that vary from white to pink, red, or purple. The flower clusters make the tree popular with nectar-feeding birds.

Introduced from Australia
Grown in the U.S. from California east to Arizona
Grows 33–100 ft (10-30 m) tall
Leaves around 8 in (20 cm) long

Silver Dollar Tree
(Eucalyptus cinerca)

This eucalyptus is known for its round, bright, blue-white leaves. The branches are often used by florists for the silvery leaves.

Introduced from Australia
Grown in the southern and southwestern U.S.
Up to 60 ft (18 m) tall—Leaves 4–5 in (10–12.5 cm) long

Russian Olive
(Elaeagnus angustifolia)

Russian olive has leaves, twigs, and fruits that are covered with silvery scales. Even its yellow, bell-shaped flowers are silvery on the outside. In spite of its name, Russian olive is not related to the olive tree, although it does produce sweet fruits that contain a single stone. Waxwings, robins, pheasants, and other birds feed on them.

Introduced from southern Europe and Asia
Planted across southern Canada and the U.S.
Grows up to 20 ft (6 m) tall, but is often a shrub
Leaves 1½–3¼ in (4–8 cm) long

Pacific Madrona
(Arbutus menziesii)

This tree, also called madrone, grows in woods on low mountains, and in towns, parks, and gardens. New shoots are light green, but turn to reddish-brown as the bark becomes thicker. The underside of the leaves is blue-white. The white clusters of flowers are followed by berries, which are orange and then scarlet.

Native to the Pacific Coast from
Vancouver Island to Los Angeles, Calif.
Grows up to 100 ft (30 m) tall
Leaves 2–6 in (5–15 cm) long

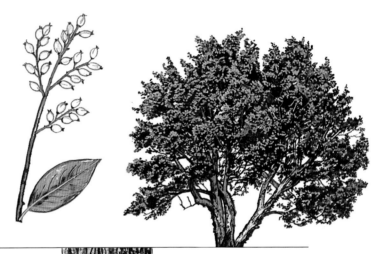

California Laurel
(Umbrellularia californica)

Like gum trees, California laurel has leaves that smell spicy when crushed. Do not sniff them for too long though, or the smell may give you a headache.

Native to the West Coast
of the U.S.
Grows up to 80 ft (24 m) tall
Leaves 2–5 in (5–12.5 cm) long

Palms & Palmlike Trees

Palms are easy to recognize. Most have a single trunk with no branches and large, spreading leaves. They differ from other trees because they have no heartwood and show no annual rings in their trunks.

Cabbage Palm
(Sabal palmetto)

Cabbage palms have fan-shaped leaves, which spread out around the top of the trunk. The leaves are dark green and shiny, and are deeply cut into many slender strips. The fragrant, white flowers are followed by clusters of shiny, black berries. The leaves are made into baskets and hats, and the leafstalks into brooms. The trunks are used for wharf pilings, docks, and posts.

Native to Florida and the southeastern coast of the U.S. Widely planted in streets and parks in southern and southwestern towns
Grows up to 90 ft (27 m) tall
Leaves 5–8 ft (1.5–2.5 m) long

Chusan Palm
(Trachycarpus fortunei)

This palm can grow in much colder climates than other palms. Its fanlike leaves give it another name—Chinese fan palm. The tree's trunk is hairy and scaly.
Introduced from China
Planted in parts of California and Washington state in the U.S.
Grows up to 45 ft (14 m) tall
Leaves 4 ft (1.2 m) wide

California Washingtonia
(Washingtonia filifera)

This tree is also called California palm. It is easy to recognize by its green leaves, which rise out of a frill of dead leaves around the top of the trunk. The trunk is gray or reddish brown and smoother than other palms. The clusters of yellow flowers are up to 12 inches (30 centimeters) long. The fruits are long clusters of black berries.
Native to the southwestern U.S.
Grows up to 60 ft (18 m) tall
Leaves 5 ft long (1.5 m) on 5 ft (1.5 m) stalks

Queen Palm
(Syagrus romanzoffiana)

This tree is easily recognized by the dark gray rings on its pale gray trunk. Its leaves look soft and feathery.
Introduced from South America
Grows up to 60 ft (18 m) tall
Leaves 15 ft (4.5 m) long

Joshua Tree
(Yucca brevifolia)

The Joshua tree may be identified by its many short, upturned branches. It was named by the Mormons, who thought it looked like a man lifting his arms to heaven. Joshua tree is a yucca, not a palm. Its daggerlike leaves end in a sharp point and are clustered at the end of the branches. The white flowers give way to brown fruits holding many seeds.

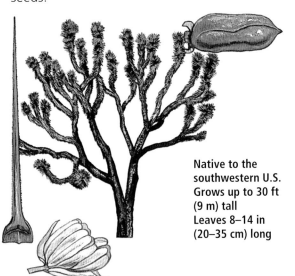

Native to the southwestern U.S.
Grows up to 30 ft (9 m) tall
Leaves 8–14 in (20–35 cm) long

Date Palm
(Phoenix dactylifera)

Date palms have gray-green leaves in the shape of long plumes with many stiff leaflets. Look for the bunches of sweet, dark brown dates for which the tree is cultivated in Florida and California. You will also see many of them in the streets of Phoenix, Arizona, and the city itself shares the tree's genus name, Phoenix.
Introduced from North Africa and western Asia
Planted in hot, dry parts of Florida, California, and Arizona
Grows up to 100 ft (30 m) tall
Leaves up to 20 ft (6 m) long

Canary Island Date Palm
(Phoenix canariensis)

Canary palm is sometimes called pineapple palm because its trunk is covered with the rough scales of dropped leaf stalks, and so it looks something like the outside of a pineapple. The flowers produce datelike fruits, but they are not good to eat.
Introduced from the Canary Islands
Most common along the Gulf of Mexico and California coasts in the U.S.
Grows up to 60 ft (18 m) tall
Leaves 15–20 ft (4.5–6 m) long

More Trees Needed

When they reach a height of six feet (around 2 meters), young trees are called saplings. They can be found in parks and woods, or you can grow your own from seeds.

Choosing a tree for planting

Do you have room in your yard for a new tree? Before you rush out to plant a specially purchased tree or one of your seedlings, think about what kind of tree would best suit your yard.

Sycamore, ash, and tree of heaven grow very large very quickly. You could soon have a monster tree in your yard, blocking out the light and pushing its roots under the walls of the house, which could damage it badly. You will find that mountain ash, gray birch, and black cherry are all attractive trees that do not grow very large. Many trees are not grown from seed. They are grafted on to the stems of other trees and can only be bought from a tree nursery. They are more expensive than growing your own seedlings, but often they have been specially produced for yards.

Grown your own

1 **In autumn collect seeds** from trees like oak, ash, gray birch, and cypress.
2 **Soak the seeds overnight** then peel off their tough outer skin.

3 **Plant several seeds from one tree in a pot of compost.** Cover with more compost and water well.
4 **Leave the pots in a cool place** and wait to see what happens. Don't let the compost dry out.

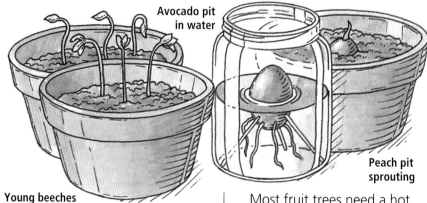

Avocado pit in water

Young beeches

Peach pit sprouting

Exotic trees

The next time you eat some fruit—apple, pear, orange, cherry, or peach—save the seeds and pits. Soak them in water for a few days, then plant a few of each kind in a small pot of compost. Water the pot well and leave in a cool place.

Avocados have large pits. Soak one in water for a week as shown above, then plant it in a pot of compost with its tip just showing above the surface.

Most fruit trees need a hot, sunny climate. If any of yours grow, put them in a hot, sunny place, or in a greenhouse. Much of the fruit we eat has few or no seeds or pits at all. The trees that produce this fruit are often grown from grafts and are not very fertile. So, don't be disappointed if these seeds do not grow.

Planting your tree

1 **Use a yard of string and two pins** to make a circle on the ground.

2 **Dig a hole about 2 feet (0.5 meter) deep.** Loosen any stones or hard earth at the bottom of the hole.
3 **Line the bottom of the hole** with leaf mold or manure to about 6 inches (15 centimeters) deep.

4 **Push a short stake or post into the hole.** This will support the tree against wind and accidents.
5 **Take the tree out of its container and hold it in place in the center of the hole.** Spread out the roots and fill in around them with a mixture of soil, compost, and sand.
6 **Press the top soil down firmly and rake it over gently.** Tie the tree to the stake with at least two plastic tree ties, which you can buy at a nursery, hardware store, or gardening center. Water the tree well and it should eventually begin to grow.

7 **Check from time to time** that the ties are not cutting into the tree. You can remove the stake after about two years.

Ask an adult to help with the digging.

Ginkgos, Yews, & Others

The trees on these two pages are all conifers, but are unusual in different ways. Most of them, for example, produce berrylike fruits instead of woody cones.

Ginkgo
(Ginkgo biloba)

The ginkgo is sometimes called a living fossil. It flourished more than 200 million years ago when dinosaurs roamed the earth, but died out everywhere except in China. It was introduced into America in the 1700's. Gingkos are easy to recognize from their fan-shaped leaves and small, soft fruits. The fruits smell awful when they rot, so usually only male trees are planted. Though the ginkgo is often included with the conifers, it is a deciduous, broadleaf tree.
**Introduced from China
Planted from Canada
to New Orleans and
west to the Pacific Coast
of the U.S.
Grows up to
80 ft (24 m) tall
Leaves 1–2 in
(2.5–5 cm) long**

Pacific Yew
(Taxus brevifolia)

This yew, also called the western yew, likes the shade of damp woods. It has flat, pointed needles and red berries like the English yew. The best way to tell them apart in the U.S. is to note whether it is growing in the West or East. Notice too the shape of the tree. Sometimes, Pacific yew grows only as a shrub.
**Native to the West Coast
of North America from
Alaska to California
Grows up to 50 ft (15 m) tall
Leaves up to
1½ in (4 cm) long**

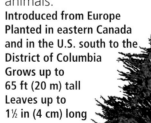

English Yew
(Taxus baccata)

Yews are very hardy trees that can live for thousands of years. Look for the red, berrylike fruits, and the single, flat, pointed needles of the yew tree, but be careful! The wood, bark, seeds, and leaves are poisonous to people and to most animals.
**Introduced from Europe
Planted in eastern Canada
and in the U.S. south to the
District of Columbia
Grows up to
65 ft (20 m) tall
Leaves up to
1½ in (4 cm) long**

Monkey Puzzle Tree
(Araucaria araucana)

Monkey puzzle, also known as the Chile pine, is easily recognized by its leaves, which grow in an interlocking spiral around the branches. The tree gets its name from the difficulty any monkey would have in climbing up through the sharp leaves. Male and female flowers usually grow on separate trees. The male cones are thin and long. The female cones are oval or round.

Introduced from Chile
Planted in western
areas from British
Columbia to California
and in the southeast
Grows up to 140 ft
(43 m) tall
Leaves 2 in
(5 cm) long

California Torreya
(Torreya californica)

California Torreya belongs to the yew family and, like yew trees, has single, flat needles. It is sometimes called California nutmeg because its fleshy fruits look like true nutmegs. The fruits have purple stripes when they are ripe and contain a hard seed.
Native to parts of California
in the U.S.
Grows up to 70 ft (21 m) tall
Leaves 1–2¾ in (2.5–7 cm) long

Nagi Podocarp
(Nageia nagi)

This tree is sometimes known as a broadleaf podocarp, because of its unusually wide leaves. The leaves of many podocarps look like those of yew, but their fruits are different from those seen on many yew trees. Some podocarps produce cones with fleshy scales, while the nagi produces green, plumlike fruits. Podocarps are also known as yellowwoods.
Native to China and Japan
Planted from South Carolina to
southern California in the U.S.
Grows up to 50 ft (15 m) tall
Leaves 2–4 ins (5–10 cm) long

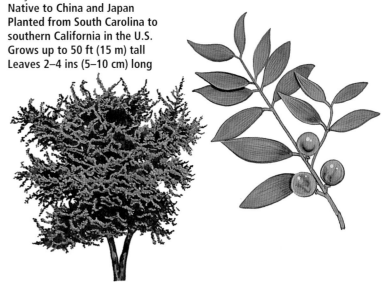

Juniper & Redcedars

All the trees on these two pages belong to the cypress family. Apart from common juniper, all cypresses have scalelike leaves. Like yews, junipers produce berrylike fruits instead of cones. Junipers can be distinguished from yews (see page 58) by their scalelike leaves and the shape of the tree.

Common Juniper
(Juniperus communis)

Juniper is the most widespread conifer in North America. Although it sometimes grows as a small tree in New England, it grows only as a shrub elsewhere.
   The whitish-blue, berrylike cones take two to three years to ripen, so some are always on the bush. Grouse, pheasants, and bobwhites feed on them. The cones are also used to flavor gin. The needles grow in clusters of three along the stems.

Native across all of Canada and parts of the U.S. with cold climates
Grows up to 25 ft (7.5 m) tall, but is usually a shrub of 1–4 ft (0.3–1.2 m)
Leaves up to ½ in (1 cm) long

Utah Juniper
(Juniperus osteosperma)

This tree is very common around the Grand Canyon and the dry areas from Wyoming to California. It is a distinctively shaped—with gray-brown, striped bark.
Native to west and southwestern U.S.
Grows up to 40 ft (12 m) tall
Leaves less than 1 in (2.5 cm) long

Meyer's Blue Juniper
(Juniperus squamata 'Meyeri')

This juniper has dense foliage of blue-green needles.
Introduced from China
Planted in yards in British Columbia, Canada, and Washington and Ohio in the U.S.
Grows up to 25 ft (7.5 m) tall
Leaves ½–1 in (1–2.5 cm) long

Eastern Redcedar
(Juniperus virginiana)

Eastern redcedar is the most common juniper tree east of the Rocky Mountains. It can stand up to extreme heat and cold. Its scalelike leaves form green twigs. The soft, berrylike cones are sweet and juicy. Waxwings and other birds like to feed on them. The trees are planted for shelter and to be harvested as Christmas trees. The wood is used to make cedar chests, fence posts, and carvings. Oil from the leaves and wood is used in medicines and perfumes. The Rocky Mountain juniper is closely related, but it grows only to the west of the prairie states.
Native to the eastern U.S.
Grows up to 60 ft (18 m) tall
Leaves ½ in (1 cm) long

The trees on this page have an aromatic and resinous smell.

Western Redcedar
(Thuja plicata)

This is a huge tree with long, flask-shaped cones that each have 10 to 12 scales. Its scalelike leaves have a fruity scent when crushed. Like the northern white-cedar, redcedar wood was used by American Indians to make canoes; it is light and strong and does not rot in water. They also used the wood for totem poles, houses, and boxes. Today, it is made into shingles (wooden roof tiles).
Native to western states from Alaska to California
Grows up to 175 ft (53 m) tall
Scalelike leaves less than 1 in (2.5 cm) long

Northern White-cedar
(Thuja occidentalis)

Northern white-cedar grows very slowly and can live for 400 years or more. Turn the yellow-green leaves over to see their pale, blue-green or yellow-green underside. When crushed, they smell bitter. There are smooth, brown cones at the ends of some shoots. American Indians used the strong, light wood to build canoes. Today, the wood is used mainly for posts and poles. The twigs are used to make cedar oil for medicines.
Native to eastern Canada and the northeastern U.S.
Grows up to 70 ft (21 m) tall
Scalelike leaves about ⅛ in (0.3 cm) long

Oriental Arborvitae
(Thuja orientalis)

The best way to identify this tree is by its shape. It often has branches sprouting from the bottom of the trunk. In China, the scented branches are used in New Year's celebrations. When the leaves are crushed, they release a scent similar to pine resin. The tree has many cones; they are blue-white in summer, but later turn dark brown. There are many different cultivars of arborvitae, including one with golden leaves. Arborvitae means "tree of life." The northern white-cedar and western red-cedar are also arborvitaes.
Introduced from China
Planted across the U.S., especially in southeastern states
Grows up to 25 ft (7.5 m) tall
Scalelike leaves about ⅛ in (0.3 cm) long

Cypresses

Some cypresses are called cedars, but you can tell they are cypresses by their scaly leaves. There are two kinds of cypress trees. "True" cypresses have big cones, and "false" cypresses have small cones and leaves in flattened sprays.

Arizona Smooth Cypress
(Cupressus arizonica)

The bark on this tree varies from smooth and peeling to rough and furrowed. The leaves are sometimes speckled with spots of white resin.
Native to Arizona and nearby states
Grows up to 70 ft (21 m) tall
Scalelike leaves about ¹⁄₁₆ in (0.1 cm) long

Incense Cedar
(Libocedrus decurrens)

This cypress is named after its sweet-smelling wood and foliage, and its oil smells like incense. It is similar in shape to the western redcedar (see page 61). But the cones of the incense cedar have only about half as many scales.
Native to Oregon, California, and Nevada
Planted elsewhere in the U.S.
Grows up to 150 ft (45 m) or more tall
Leaves ½ in (1 cm) long

Italian Cypress
(Cupressus sempervirens)

The leaves and cones of Italian cypress look much like those of Monterey cypress, but the two trees are easily distinguished by their shape. Italian cypresses grow in narrow columns, often with a pointed top.
Native to the eastern Mediterranean
Planted in the south and west of the U.S.
Grows up to 60 ft (18 m) tall
Scalelike leaves about ⅛ in (0.3 cm) long

Monterey Cypress
(Cupressus macrocarpa)

The Monterey cypress can be identified by the lemon scent of its crushed leaves. Some wild trees grow in strange shapes. The tree's long, slender branches are covered thickly with leaves that look like ropes. The cones are almost 2 inches (5 centimeters) across and are roughly round with scales that remain attached. The scales are shaped like shields. Monterey cypresses grow on cliffs along the California coast. They can stand salt spray, but not extreme cold.
Native to California
Grows up to 115 ft (35 m) tall
Scalelike leaves about ⅛ in (0.3 cm) long

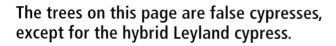

The trees on this page are false cypresses, except for the hybrid Leyland cypress.

Atlantic White Cedar
(Chamaecyparis thyoides)

This tree gets its name from its pale green leaves with white marks near their base. When crushed, they smell of ginger. The wood is so long lasting that fallen trees that have been buried for many years can still be used for lumber.

**Native to swamps on the East Coast of the U.S.
Grows up to
90 ft (27 m) tall
Scalelike leaves up to
⅛ in (0.3 cm) long**

Port-Orford-Cedar
(Chamaecyparis lawsoniana)

This tree now comes in many shapes and sizes. There are many cultivars with leaves that vary in color from blue to gray, green, and gold. The leaves of wild trees are dark green. When crushed, the leaves release a smell of parsley-scented resin. The Port-Orford has dark red male cones and bluish-green female cones growing on the same tree. In Europe it is called the Lawson cypress.

**Native to the California-Oregon border
Planted along West Coast
Grows up to 160 ft (50 m) tall
Scalelike leaves ¾ in (2 cm) long**

Alaska-Cedar
(Chamaecyparis nootkatensis)

This tree is most easily distinguished from other cypresses by the hooked spikes on its round cones. The tree itself is cone-shaped with drooping branches. When crushed, the leaves smell of turpentine. This tree can stand very cold weather and can live 1,000 years or more.

**Native to Alaska and western areas of the U.S. and Canada
Grows up to 100 ft (30 m) tall
Scalelike leaves ⅛ in (0.3 cm) long**

Leyland Cypress
(Cupressocyparis leylandii)

There are many different cultivars of Leyland cypress. These trees grow very quickly and are often planted to make a thick hedge. The Leyland cypress is a sterile hybrid of the Monterey cypress (a true cypress) and the Alaska-cedar (a false cypress).

**Grows up to
130 ft (40 m) tall
Scalelike leaves
less than 1 in
(2.5 cm) long**

Redwoods & Larches

Although they carry the names of various other trees—cedar, cypress, and fir—all the trees on this page are redwoods. Redwoods are large, beautiful trees. They have thick, fibrous, red barks and small, woody cones with scales shaped like shields.

Chinese Fir
(Cunninghamia lanceolata)

Introduced from China to the U.S.
Grows up to 60 ft (18 m) tall
Leaves 1¼–3 in (3–7.5 cm) long

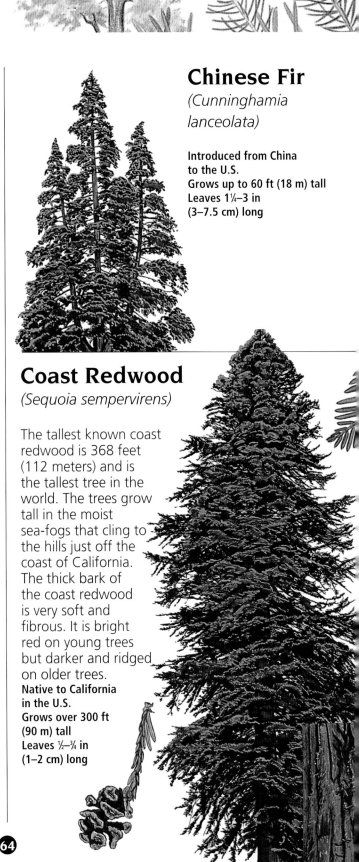

Giant Sequoia
(Sequoiadendron giganteum)

Giant sequoias are not quite the tallest trees in the world, but they are among the most massive and also the oldest. "General Sherman," a tree in Sequoia National Park in California, is 274 feet (83.5 m) tall and measures 103 feet (31.4 m) around the trunk. Giant sequoias have deep roots and thick bark, which allows them to survive gales and forest fires. In fact, sequoias need forest fires to thrive. The heat opens their cones and releases their seeds; fires also create space for new sequoias to grow. Sequoia leaves do not cling to the branches as closely as those of cypresses.

Native to California
Planted north to Vancouver, Canada
Grows up to 250 ft (76 m) tall
Leaves ¼ –⅓ in (0.5–0.7 cm) long

Coast Redwood
(Sequoia sempervirens)

The tallest known coast redwood is 368 feet (112 meters) and is the tallest tree in the world. The trees grow tall in the moist sea-fogs that cling to the hills just off the coast of California. The thick bark of the coast redwood is very soft and fibrous. It is bright red on young trees but darker and ridged on older trees.

Native to California in the U.S.
Grows over 300 ft (90 m) tall
Leaves ½–¾ in (1–2 cm) long

A Chinese fir is similar to a coast redwood. Their needles differentiate them. Chinese fir needles are much longer and broader than those of the coast redwood, and they narrow to a sharp point. There will be spiny cones and rusty, dead leaves among the bright green, new needles.

Japanese Redcedar
(Cryptomeria japonica)

The leaves of this tree are sharp and scaly and cover the shoots. It has horizontal branches, which sometimes form billowing clumps.
Introduced from China and Japan
Planted on the East and West coasts of the U.S.
Grows up to 100 ft (30 m) tall
Leaves about ½ in (1 cm) long

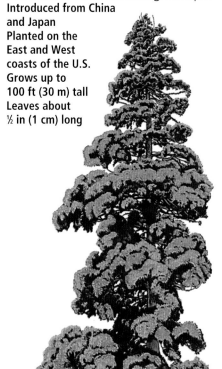

The trees below belong to the larch family and are deciduous—that is, they lose their leaves in winter.

Western Larch
(Larix occidentalis)

Western larch is the biggest larch of all. Its bright green needles grow in rosettes on side twigs and singly on main twigs. The needles turn golden-yellow before they drop in fall. Look too for the whiskery cones.

Native to the Rocky Mountains from British Columbia to Montana
Grows up to 150 ft (45 m) tall
Leaves up to 2 in (5 cm) long

Tamarack
(Larix laricina)

Also called the eastern larch, this is one of the most northerly conifers in North America. It grows across Canada and as far north as trees can grow. The needles are bright green and grow in rosettes or singly. The tree has scaly, pink-brown bark. American Indians used the slender roots to bind birch bark for their canoes.
Native to Canada, and the upper Midwestern and northeastern U.S.
Grows up to 60 ft (18 m) tall
Leaves 1 in (2.5 cm) long

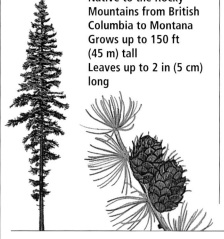

Baldcypress
(Taxodium distichum)

Baldcypress lives in wet soil, along riverbanks, and beside lakes. When its roots are submerged in water, it grows "knees"—broad pillars 20 yards (18 meters) or more from the tree, which reach about 5 feet (1.5 meters) high and through which the roots can breathe oxygen. It is sometimes called the "wood eternal" because it does not rot. This wood has been used to build bridges, docks, boats, and warehouses.
Native to the southeastern U.S., and up the Mississippi River to Illinois
Grows up to 120 ft (36 m) tall
Leaves ½–¾ in (1–2 cm) long

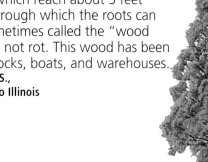

Firs & True Cedars

Fir trees have single, blunt needles and, except for the Douglas-fir, their cones stand upright. The true cedars shown here also have upright cones.

White Fir
(Abies concolor)

The needles of the white fir are blue-green with lighter stripes on both sides of the leaf. When crushed, they smell of lemons. They curve upward from the upper twigs. Cones of the white fir are green, purple, or yellow.

Native to Colorado, New Mexico, and areas westward
Grows up to 130 ft (40 m) tall
Leaves 2 in (5 cm) long

Grand Fir
(Abies grandis)

Grand firs grow very quickly and are one of the tallest silver firs. The grand fir can be identified by its flat sprays of needles, which smell of tangerines when crushed. It is hard to see the cones on this fir, as they grow only near the crown of the tree. The cones break up on the tree, so they are not found on the ground.

Native to the west coast of Canada and in the U.S.
Grows up to 200 ft (60 m) tall
Leaves 2 in (5 cm) long

Pacific Silver Fir
(Abies amabilis)

Another name for this fir is beautiful fir, and it certainly lives up to its name. Like the balsam fir, the Pacific silver is full of resin. The leaves are shiny dark green above and bright white underneath.

Native to the western coast from British Columbia, Canada to Oregon in the U.S.
Grows to 150 ft (45 m) and sometimes taller
Leaves 1½ in (4 cm) long

Balsam Fir
(Abies balsamea)

This fir grows into a narrow, pointed crown and is often used as a Christmas tree. The cones are purple at first but turn brown as they ripen. The tree's needles are dark green above and have two narrow, white bands below. When rubbed, the needles release the aromatic scent of balsam. The tree forms large blisters of resin in the bark. This resin, called Canada balsam, has been used for mounting microscopic specimens.

Native to Canada and the U.S.
Grows up to 60 ft (18 m) tall
Leaves 1–1½ in (2.5–4 cm) long

Cedars are large, magnificent trees with needles that grow singly or in rosettes.

Douglas-Fir
(Pseudotsuga menziesii)

The Douglas-fir is not a true fir. It has hanging cones and is similar to the hemlocks (see page 69). The tree is one of the world's largest, and it covers huge areas of land along the Pacific coast. Douglas-firs growing inland in the Rockies are smaller trees with smaller cones. The wood is strong, durable, and valuable. It is often used in construction.
Native to the western U.S. and Canada
Grows up to 250 ft (76 m) tall
Leaves 1 in (2.5 cm) long

Atlas Cedar
(Cedrus atlantica)

This North African tree grows in parks and gardens in the United States as an ornamental. The most common variety has gray-blue needles. The needles of the Atlas cedar form large clumps. Its cones can be more than 3 inches (7.5 centimeters) long and grow upright. In fall, pollen-bearing structures can be seen.
Introduced from North Africa
Planted on the East and West coasts of the U.S.
Grows up to 80 ft (24 m) tall
Leaves 1 in (2.5 cm) long

Deodar Cedar
(Cedrus deodara)

Deodar cedar can be differentiated from Atlas cedar by its branches, which spread downward to the ground. Its new, young shoots also hang down. And the dark green leaves of the deodar cedar are longer than those of the Atlas cedar.
Introduced from the Himalaya
Planted in the U.S. in the East, Midwest, and along the West Coast
Grows up to 80 ft (24 m) tall
Needlelike leaves 2 in (5 cm) long

Spruces & Hemlocks

Spruces have single, sharp needles and hanging cones. The trees are cone-shaped, too. Hemlocks are similar, but they have smaller cones and soft, blunt-tipped, flattened needles that are joined to the branch by small woody stalks.

Norway Spruce
(Picea abies)

This strong European tree is often pyramid-shaped, but this varies with its location. It is planted for shade and, on both sides of the U.S.-Canadian border, to give shelter for crops and homes from the winds that sweep across the prairies. The hanging cones are up to 6 inches (15 centimeters) long, longer than those of any other spruce.

Introduced from Europe
Planted widely in southeastern Canada, and the northeast, Rocky Mountains, and West Coast of the U.S.
Grows up to 80 ft (24 m) tall
Needles ½–1 in (1–2.5 cm) long

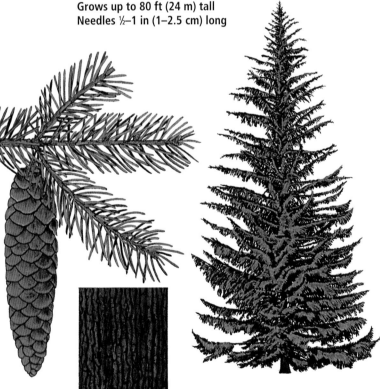

White Spruce
(Picea glauca)

This is Canada's most important commercial tree. It is made into pulpwood and paper and is also used to make musical instruments such as violins and pianos. The needles on the white spruce are shorter than those of the Norway spruce and smell of skunk when crushed. The white spruce has shiny, light brown cones with smooth, thin scales. The cones drop to the ground as they ripen.

Native to Canada, and the northern U.S., including Alaska
Grows up to 150 ft (45 m) tall
Needles ½–¾ in (1–2 cm) long

Engelmann Spruce
(Picea engelmannii)

This spruce is similar to white spruce. It grows from western Canada through the mountains to New Mexico and Arizona in the U.S. It is often planted along roadsides and in yards and parks. It has longer, softer needles than the white spruce. The ripe cones are light brown with toothed edges to the scales.

Native to the eastern Rocky Mountains
Grows up to 100 ft (30 m) tall
Needles ¾–1 in (2 –2.5 cm) long

Red Spruce
(Picea rubens)

Red spruce is related to black spruce and sometimes forms a hybrid with it. Red spruce has reddish-brown cones and bark while black spruce has dull gray cones and bark. The red spruce has bright, grassy-green needles that are short and wiry. They have white lines on one side.

Native to eastern Canada and in the eastern U.S.
Grows up to 80 ft (24 m) tall—Needles ½ in (1 cm) long

Black Spruce
(Picea mariana)

This tree is called black spruce because it looks dark from a distance. An old black spruce is unmistakable with its tall, thin shape and open-spaced branches. In winter, snow presses the lowest branches down to the ground. There they take root and begin to grow, creating a ring of saplings around the old tree. The dull gray cones are egg-shaped and numerous. The black spruce has small, thin needles.

Native to Canada, and to Alaska and the northeast of the U.S.
Grows up to 60 ft (18 m) tall
Needles ½ in (1 cm) long

Western & Eastern Hemlock
(Tsuga heterophylla and *Tsuga canadensis)*

The eastern, or Canadian, hemlock is smaller than the western, growing only to about 70 feet (21 meters) tall. American colonists used to make tea from the leafy twigs of eastern hemlock, found from the Great Lakes to the Appalachians. Both trees feature paler bands of color on the underside of the leaves. The shoots and leaves of eastern hemlock are droopy, while the western hemlock has longer needles.

Native to West or East of North America
Western: up to 200 ft (60 m) tall
Needles about 1/2 in (2 cm) long

Sitka Spruce
(Picea sitchensis)

Sitka spruces are the biggest spruces in the world and are felled for their timber. The Sitka is one of the prickliest spruces. Its needles are hard and stiff and have sharp points. It has scaly, gray bark and light brown cones with papery scales.

Native to the west coast of North America
Grows up to 300 ft (90 m) tall
Needles ⅝–1 in (1.5–2.5 cm) long

Trees & People

We need trees. The roots of trees hold the soil and stop it from being blown or washed away. Trees drink in huge quantities of water and slowly release it back into the air through a process called transpiration. They help to clean the air by absorbing carbon dioxide, a gas released when coal, for example, is burned. In addition, trees add beauty to our lives.

Planting trees that will be allowed to grow for hundreds of years is an important thing we can do for the future.

Befriend a tree

You can make a record of all the different kinds of trees you recognize or you can concentrate on just one tree, using many of the activities in this book to get to know it really well (see opposite).

You can also help to save trees by recycling paper and buying products that encourage the continued growth of rain forest trees.

Acid Rain

Automobiles, factories, and power stations release waste gases into the air. Many of these gases are acidic and combine with the water in the air to produce acid rain, snow, or sleet. Wind and air currents can carry acid rain clouds for hundreds of miles before they fall as rain. Acid rain has affected parts of eastern North America, Scandinavia, and central Europe. Acid rain harms a tree by slowly causing its leaves to die. Acid rain changes the composition of the soil and can make it harder for trees to get nutrients. Experts believe that acid rain and fog damage leaves and make trees more sensitive to cold weather. Acid rain also damages bodies of water and the animals who depend on them.

Testing for acid rain

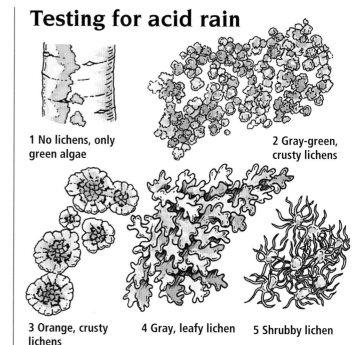

1 No lichens, only green algae

2 Gray-green, crusty lichens

3 Orange, crusty lichens

4 Gray, leafy lichen

5 Shrubby lichen

Lichens are very simple organisms that grow on the bark of trees and stones. They are very sensitive to air pollution. Look at the lichens growing in your area and compare them with the pictures above. #1 is from a high pollution area, but #5 is from an area that has hardly any pollution at all.

A tree diary

Choose a tree that you see every day and keep track of it for a whole year. Write down when it flowers, when new leaves form, when the flowers turn to fruit, and when the new buds appear.

- **Make a rubbing of its bark** and collect some of its leaves to press. Collect some seeds and see if you can grow a new tree from them.
- **Measure its height** at the beginning and end of the year. How much did it grow?
- **Measure its girth** to find out its age (see page 19).
- **Look for birds, insects, and other animals** that use the tree for food or shelter.

May 12 – Littleleaf Linden

Green fly were hatching on leaves.

Leaf from lower branches.

Sparrow first seen building nest in top branches at 11-00 am.

Still building at 2-00 pm.

Recycling paper

By recycling paper, you save living trees from being cut down to make new paper. Collect cardboard, newspapers, and other good quality waste paper, and take it regularly to be recycled.

Buy products made from recycled paper whenever possible.

Two-needled Pines

Pine trees are easy to recognize from their long, thin needles, which grow in bundles of two, three, or five. The trees on these two pages all have two needles in each bundle. The shape of the tree and the cones can be used to differentiate the types of two-needled pines.

Lodgepole Pine
(Pinus contorta var. *latifolia)*

Lodgepole pines and shore pines (*Pinus contorta*) both have prickly cones. Shore pines are usually small, bushy trees that grow along the coast. Lodgepoles are taller and grow inland in the mountains. The cones may stay closed on the tree for years until a fire sweeps through the area. Then the cones open and a new generation of trees grows.

**Native to the West of the U.S.
Grows up to 80 ft (24 m) tall
Needles 2½ in (6.5 cm) long**

Austrian Pine
(Pinus nigra)

In Europe this tree is called black pine. You can recognize it from its scaly, dark gray bark, its thick, spreading branches, and its rounded crown. The tree's dark green needles are long, stiff, and shiny and are clustered thickly around the stem. Austrian pine makes a good town tree. It is tough and fast-growing, and it does not mind city smoke and dust.

**Introduced from central and southern Europe
Planted across the U.S.
Grows up to 60 ft (18 m) tall
needles 3½–6 in (9–15 cm) long**

Red Pine
(Pinus resinosa)

Red pine has reddish bark like that of Scotch pine. Its needles can be used to tell them apart. Red pine's needles are long and ooze a strong-smelling sap when broken. Red pine is sometimes called Norway pine, but this is a confusing name for a native tree that probably arose because early explorers confused it with the Norway spruce.

**Native to southeastern Canada and the northeastern U.S.
Grows up to 80 ft (24 m) tall
Needles 4½–6½ in (11.5–16.5 cm) long**

Scotch Pine
(Pinus sylvestris)

Scotch pine can be differentiated from other pines (except red pine) by its dark red or pink bark, and its twisted pairs of blue-gray needles. This pine has small, egg-shaped, woody cones. It is grown for shelter, as an ornamental tree, and for Christmas trees.

Introduced from Europe and Asia
Now grows wild in southeastern
Canada and the northeastern U.S.
Grows up to 70 ft (21 m) tall
Needles 1½–2¾ in (4–7 cm) long

Jack Pine
(Pinus banksiana)

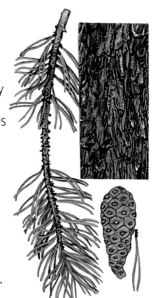

Jack pines have very short, shiny green needles. The long cones end in a curved point. The cones stay closed on the tree for many years. Like lodgepole pine cones, these cones are released and grow after a forest fire has burned the parent trees. The cones of jack pine point outward, whereas those of lodgepole point inward.

Native to Canada and the northern U.S.
Grows up to 70 ft (21 m) tall
Needles ¾–1½ in (2–4 cm) long

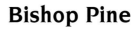

Spruce Pine
(Pinus glabra)

Spruce pine has roundish cones and thin, flexible needles. It features pale gray bark, which is smooth on young trees but becomes darker and furrowed on older trees.

Native to the southern U.S.
Grows up to 90 ft (27 m) tall
Needles 1½–4 in (4–10 cm) long

Bishop Pine
(Pinus muricata)

Bishop pine often has a wide, domed crown with rough branches. The tree has clusters of three to five cones. They are even spikier than those of lodgepole pine and stay closed for many years.

Native to California
in the U.S.
Grows up to 80 ft
(24 m) tall
Needles 6 in (15 cm) long

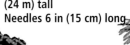

Three-needled Pines

The pine trees on these two pages have needles mainly in bundles of three.

Ponderosa Pine
(Pinus ponderosa)

Ponderosa pine is the most common pine in the Rocky Mountains. They were even more plentiful at one time, but many were cleared by logging, for grazing, or by fire, leaving vast areas of semi-desert and scrub. This is a handsome tree with long needles. The needles usually grow in bundles of three, but some grow in pairs. The bark is pinky-brown and flakes off in lobed segments that look like the pieces of a jigsaw puzzle. The tree's prickly cones are about 4–5 inches (10–12.5 centimeters) long.
**Native to the Rocky Mountains into southern Canada
Grows up to
130 ft (40 m) tall
Needles up to
9 in (23 cm) long**

Knobcone Pine
(Pinus attenuata)

Knobcone pines have bright grass-green needles and get rough, scaly bark as the trees age. The tree features tightly closed cones hanging down close to the stems.
**Native to Oregon and California
Grows up to 80 ft (24 m) tall
Needles 3–7 in (7.5–18 cm) long**

Monterey Pine
(Pinus radiata)

Monterey pine has shiny green needles and heavily loaded branches thick with cones. The large cones may stay on the tree for many years.
**Native to southern
California in the U.S.
Grows up to
100 ft (30 m) tall
Needles 6 in
(15 cm) long**

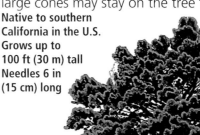

Shortleaf Pine
(Pinus echinata)

The needles of shortleaf pine grow in pairs as well as in bundles of three, but they are much shorter than those of ponderosa pine. Shortleaf pine is cut for its timber. The wood is used in construction, for plywood, and for making paper.
Native to the southeastern U.S.
Grows up to 100 ft (30 m) tall
Needles 2–4 in (5–10 cm) long

Colorado Pinyon Pine
(Pinus edulis)

Colorado pinyons are small, bushy trees with rough, irregular cones. This pinyon species has pairs of needles, while other pinyons have one, three, or four. Pine nuts are the seeds of the pinyon pine and are used in American southwestern cooking.
Native to the southwestern U.S.
Grows up to 35 ft (10 m) tall—Needles ¾–1½ in (2–4 cm) long

Pitch Pine
(Pinus rigida)

Pitch pine can be distinguished from other pines by the tufts of needles that sprout from its trunk. Its yellow-green needles are stiff and twisted. Pitch pines are now cut for their timber and for their pulp, which is made into paper. They were once valued for their resin. Colonists made turpentine, tar, and axle grease from the resin.
Native to the northeastern U.S.
Grows up to 60 ft (18 m) tall
Needles 3–5 in (7.5–12.5 cm) long

Loblolly Pine
(Pinus taeda)

This tree grows alongside roads, or in plantations where it is cut for its timber and for making into paper. "Loblolly" is an old word for mud puddle—this tree grows in wetter ground than other pines. Its thick bark is blackish-gray with deep, scaly ridges. Its cones open on the tree.
Native to the southeastern U.S.
Grows up to 100 ft (30 m) tall
Needles 5–9 in (12.5–23 cm) long

Five-needled Pines

The trees on these two pages have needles in bundles of five.

Sugar Pine
(Pinus lambertiana)

The sugar pine is among the tallest pines in the world and produces the largest cones, up to 30 inches (76 centimeters) long. Like the white pines (opposite), many of these trees are killed by blister rust.

Native to Oregon and California in the U.S.
Grows up to 160 ft (50 m) tall
Needles 4 in (10 cm) long

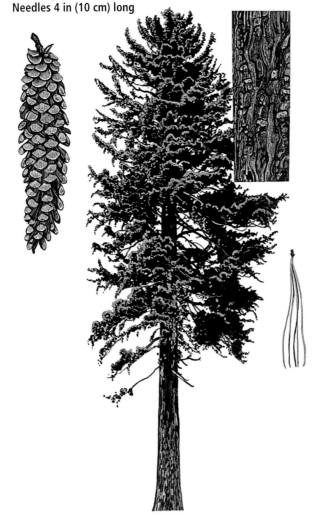

Limber Pine
(Pinus flexilis)

This tall, slender pine grows high in the Rockies. The young shoots are so flexible, they can be tied in knots without breaking. The cones are about 6 inches (15 centimeters) long and have thick scales. They contain large, edible seeds.

Native to the Rocky Mountains
Up to 50 ft (15 m) tall
Needles up to 3½ in (9 cm) long

Rocky Mountain Bristlecone Pine
(Pinus aristata)

Some trees of this species are among the oldest living things in the world and have lived as long as 4,600 years. This pine features tufts of five needles; the needles press close to the shoot and curve inward.

Native to the Rocky Mountains
Grows up to 70 ft (21 m) tall
Needles up to 1½ in (4 cm) long

Whitebark Pine

(Pinus albicaulis)

Like the limber pine, whitebark pines grow high in the mountains. They can be distinguished by their cones. Those of the whitebark pine are short and squat. They do not open, but fall off the tree, where birds pick out the seeds.

Native to the Rocky Mountains
Grows up to 50 ft (15 m) tall
Needles up to 2¾ in (7 cm) long

Western White Pine

(Pinus monticola)

Western white pine has much longer cones than Eastern white pine. They are about 8 to 9 inches (20–23 centimeters) long and slightly curved. The bark is gray-green and on young trees it is smooth. On older trees the bark is rougher with scaly plates. Many older trees are killed by a fungal disease called blister rust.

Native to the West Coast and western mountains of the U.S.
Grows up to 175 ft (55 m) tall
Needles 4 in (10 cm) long

Eastern White Pine

(Pinus strobus)

This five-needled pine is the state tree of Maine. It is the largest conifer in the northeast. The tree's needles are blue-green and the long, narrow cones are yellow-brown.

Native to eastern Canada and the northeastern U.S.
Grows up to 100 ft (30 m) tall
Needles 2½–5 in (6.5–12.5 cm) long

Find Out More

Glossary

bract: modified and often scalelike leaf found at the base of a flower or fruit

broadleaf: tree that has broad, flat leaves

burr: roundish growth, like a wart, on a tree's trunk

canopy: extent of the branches of a tree

catkin: drooping cluster of flowers

chlorophyll: green substance in plants that takes in light energy for use in photosynthesis

compound leaf: one large leaf made of several small leaflets

conifer: tree or shrub that has long, hard leaves (needles) and produces cones for fruit; usually evergreen

crinkly: twisted leaves, as in the holly

crown: mass of branches and twigs at the top of a tree

deciduous: tree that sheds its leaves in the autumn and is leafless for part of the year

evergreen: tree or shrub that sheds and replaces its leaves gradually all the year round and is never leafless

fungus: plantlike organism that grows on living or dead matter

grafting: placing of a shoot or bud from one plant into a slit in another plant, so that the shoot or bud will grow as part of the second plant

greenhouse: building with glass roofs and sides where the temperature and moisture are kept at the best levels for growing plants

gymnosperm: plant in which the seeds are not enclosed in fruit

leaflets: small leaves that are grouped together to form one big compound leaf, as in the ash tree

lobed: leaf that has its edges deeply divided, as in the maple tree

naturalized: species that was originally planted in one area, but now grows wild in another area

native: species that originated in a particular place

needle: leaf of a conifer

palmate: leaf that has lobes or leaflets all coming from one central point, as in the maple or horse chestnut tree

photosynthesis: process by which plants use the energy of sunlight, together with water and carbon dioxide, to make their own food

resin: sticky sap produced by certain trees, such as fir and pine

rosette: circular needle formation, as in larches

sap: sticky liquid that a tree uses to carry food to and from its roots and leaves

sapling: young tree

transpiration: process by which plants or other organisms release water vapor from a surface, such as from a leaf

variegated: leaf with more than one color

vein: the rib of a leaf

Organizations

The objective of the organization **American Forests** is the proper management of forest lands; the group publishes *American Forests* magazine. Contact: American Forests, P.O. Box 2000, Washington, D.C. 20013; (202) 955–4500.
http://www.americanforests.org

In Canada, the **Canadian Forest Service** is the best starting point. Write to: Canadian Forest Service, Natural Resources Canada, 580 Booth Street, 8th Floor, Ottawa, Ontario K1A 0E4; (613) 947-7341.
http://www.nrcan-rncan.gc.ca/cfs-scf/index_e.html

The **National Arbor Day Foundation** is dedicated to the planting and preservation of trees, from street trees to tropical forests. Write to: National Arbor Day Foundation, 100 Arbor Avenue, Nebraska City, Nebraska 68410.
http://www.arborday.org

For information about U.S. national parks, contact: **National Park Service,** 1849 C Street NW, Washington, D.C. 20240; (202) 208-6843.
http://www.nps.gov

The goal of the **Nature Conservancy** is to preserve unique and threatened habitats, many of them forested. Contact: Nature Conservancy, 4245 North Fairfax Drive, Suite 100, Arlington, Virginia 22203-1606; (703) 841-5300.
http://nature.org

For information about U.S. national forests, contact: **USDA Forest Service,** 1400 Independence Avenue SW, Washington, D.C. 20250-0002; (202) 205-8333.
http://www.fs.fed.us

Index

Additional Resources

America's Forests Frank J. Staub (Carolrhoda, 1999).

The Audubon Society Field Guide to North American Trees (2 volumes) Elbert L. Little (Knopf, 1980).

Encyclopedia of North American Trees Sam Benvie (Firefly Books, 2000).

The Illustrated Encyclopedia of Trees David More and John White (Timber Press, 2002).

North American Landscape Trees Arthur L. Jacobson (Ten Speed, 1996).

Science Project Ideas About Trees Robert Gardner (Enslow, 1997).

Trees: Their Natural History Peter Thomas (Cambridge, 2000).

Trees of North America C. Frank Brockman (St. Martin's, 2001).

Trees of the Northern United States and Canada John L. Farrar (Iowa State University Press, 1995).

Index

See *World Book's Science & Nature Guides Resources & Cumulative Index* volume for an explanation of the system used by scientists to classify living things.